VISIBILITY TODAY

EXPERTS SHARE TIPS TO HELP YOU BE SEEN, HEARD, AND SHINE!

COMPILED BY
REBECCA HALL GRUYTER

#1 INTERNATIONAL BEST SELLING AUTHOR

Visibility Today
Experts share tips to help you be seen, heard, and SHINE!

Copyright © 2024 by Rebecca Hall Gruyter

RHG Media Productions
21519 Knoll Way,
Castro Valley, CA 94546

All rights reserved. No part of this publication may be reproduced distributed or transmitted in any form or by any means including photocopying recording or other electronic or mechanical means without proper written permission of author or publisher, except in the case of brief quotations embodied in critical reviews and certain other noncommercial uses permitted by copyright law.

ISBN 978-1-7374041-5-6 (paperback)

Visit us on line at www.YourPurposeDrivenPractice.com
Printed in the United States of America.

Contents

Preface	by Rebecca Hall Gruyter, Compiler	5

Section 1: Visibility Today

Chapter 1: You First	by Mary Struzinsky	11
Chapter 2: Create the Momentum	by Rebecca Hall Gruyter	21
Chapter 3: Business Magic With the Energetic Feng Shui™ System	by Deborah Wiener	27

Section 2: Be Visible

Chapter 4: Amplifying Authentic Voices: The Power of Video in Building Personal Branding	by Maureen Ryan Blake	37
Chapter 5: Actionable Advice to Improve Your Online Visibility	by Mike O'Connor	47
Chapter 6: Interview Like a Pro	by Rebecca Hall Gruyter	57

Section 3: Grow Your Visibility

Chapter 7: Authors, Keep the Momentum Going   by Rebecca Hall Gruyter   69

Chapter 8: Fast-Track Your Success With Anthologies   by Rebecca Hall Gruyter   77

Chapter 9: Show Hosting Tips for Success   by Rebecca Hall Gruyter   85

Quotes to Inspire You   93

Closing Thoughts   by Rebecca Hall Gruyter, Compiler   105

Preface

Thank you for leaning into this powerful anthology! We are honored and excited to bring you this powerful book featuring experts who are committed to helping you embrace *Visibility Today*. We want to support you in tapping into the wisdom we have discovered and believe will empower and support you on your journey.

Our vision is to have our experts share insights, tips and tools we have discovered to support and empower you on your journey. We know that life is not a solo journey, and by coming together, our goal is to help you step further and more powerfully into your gifts, talents and abilities. Together, as we lift each other up, we are all able to grow, reach more people, and have a greater impact than we do trying to do everything on our own.

In each chapter, our authors will equip and empower you to step forward more fully. We believe this book is a living and interactive book that will speak wisdom, encouragement and power into your life. We want to invite you to pause, take a deep breath, and be ready to receive these powerful chapters so they can ignite a fire in you, inspire courage in you, and focus you on stepping fully into bringing forward the gift of who you are and all that you are called to be. Enjoy the inspirational quotes woven throughout the book to inspire, encourage and motivate you.

Here is how to get the most out of this powerful book. The book is divided into three sections, each designed to meet you exactly where you are and to support you in each step of your journey. **In the first section, Visibility Today,** you'll discover more about how visibility works in today's market. **In the second section, Be Visible,** our experts share how to be visible. **In the third section, Grow Your Visibility,** we share how to grow and expand your visibility to increase your impact and reach more people. At the end of each powerful chapter, you will find the author's biography and contact information. We encourage you to "friend" and follow those authors with whom you feel a powerful resonance and connection so that they can continue to pour into you and support you on your journey in life.

Now the next step is yours. Drink in the insights, tips and wisdom that are within these pages to serve, support and inspire you. Take the time to pause, read and reflect. Listen to the powerful messages of hope that are waiting for you within the pages of this book. It's not an accident that you purchased this book and are opening it to read. We invite you to lean in and truly receive the messages and wisdom that will speak to your heart and soul that you will find in these transformational and dynamic pages. Enjoy this rich collection of wisdom, insight and encouragement being provided by our amazing authors. We can't wait to see you embrace *Visibility Today* and SHINE!

Rebecca Hall Gruyter, Compiler
Founder/owner of Your Purpose Driven Practice and CEO of RHG Media Productions

Acknowledgments

When writing an anthology, it takes many voices willing to join together to bring forth the book in a powerful and united way. It has been such an honor and privilege to work with this amazing group of experts and influencers. We want to thank these amazing leaders for trusting us to bring forth and share their powerful stories.

Thank you to our amazing teams, communities, families, God, and friends for leaning in, cheering us on, and saying yes to help us bring this book forward so powerfully. It takes many hearts and spirits coming together, bringing their gifts and talents to the mix, to bring something like this book forward in multiple formats. We thank the full team, community, authors and readers for leaning in to support us in bringing this powerful book to the world. You make the journey brilliant by being on it with us.

SECTION 1:

Visibility Today

Chapter 1
You First
by Mary Struzinsky

I remember sitting in the parking lot of the doctor's office, on the phone with my husband, and crying so hard that he couldn't understand me. All I could think of was wanting to still be a good mom to my three daughters.

I was at the eye doctor because something was blocking the vision in my left eye, and after hours of stressful tests, they suspected I had multiple sclerosis. After months of more tests and seeing a neurologist, the diagnosis was an inflamed nerve in my brain brought on by chronic stress. I went on to have other inflammatory and neurological issues until it finally hit me that **I was so busy taking care of everyone else that I was shortening my life expectancy.** Then I wouldn't be able to take care of anyone.

I had been working as an executive director of a national human service agency, getting promoted as the company grew, and I always thought I would retire from there. It was a long, hard decision, but I quit my job and became a corporate dropout.

I went back to private practice, where I had a reasonable schedule, and started working on my physical and emotional health. I had been a licensed therapist for thirty-plus years, and I had to ask myself what was going on with me *internally*. The truth was, there were still some subconscious beliefs going back to my childhood that were driving me to feel that **a "good girl" would not put herself first.**

After working on my own limiting beliefs and prioritizing myself, all my health issues stabilized or reversed. My marriage of more than twenty-five years became the best it had ever been. My children were proud of me, business was good, and I had a wait list of clients.

But that would not be the end of the emotional work I had to do for myself.

I specialized in healing trauma, and, not surprisingly, I kept seeing women like me: exhausted and depleted and feeling like they were deficient for not being able to do it all. Past trauma was playing out in their adult lives, showing up as perfectionism, procrastination, and people-pleasing. **It wasn't from working too many hours but from not feeling worthy or deserving enough to put themselves first.** I knew I could help, and I felt called to get my message out to more women.

I hired a business coach to help me move from a brick-and-mortar business to an online business. Boy, that was a learning curve! My clients were having good outcomes, and I loved the work, but it was taking me longer than I wanted to grow this side of my business. I needed more people to know I existed, to know I had solutions for them. I threw myself into learning about speaking, podcasting, writing, building a website, posting on social media, creating a digital course, and the list goes on.

What happened next really surprised me.

I struggled to do it. I mean, I had done most of this before. I was used to speaking in front of large groups of people. I had marketed a business before. I had to network all the time as an executive director. I had been the boss of numerous people. I didn't think I had a confidence issue.

My business coach noticed my resistance, too. She told me I was playing too small. I had a physical response in my body that was very uncomfortable anytime I thought about growing my business. It wasn't until we began talking about my needing to hire an assistant that I knew what the issue was. The thought of hiring anyone triggered me.

I knew why I was playing so small. I didn't want to be visible. I didn't want my business to grow. What if it grew and I had to hire people? What if I got busy? What if it meant I would suffer from burnout again and feel trapped? I didn't want to give up my balance and freedom.

That was the subconscious message playing in my brain, and I didn't know it. I was afraid to attract a lot of clients and have a thriving business because it would mean sacrificing my free time and my health.

See, even though I am a therapist, I was unaware of my subconscious thoughts. I needed the awareness before I could change the belief. Once I knew what was holding me back, then I could change it. I could think of ways to grow my business and remember I was in charge. I could grow my business and have fun! It could look how I wanted it to, and it did not have to mean I would suffer from burnout again.

This experience, coupled with the embrace of core beliefs like "I am worthy enough to prioritize my self-care," propelled me toward defining my business vision and setting concrete goals.

I reminded myself that if I didn't make myself visible and tell people about my solutions, then *I was preventing someone from having a transformation.* That year, I started an online community for women working on their self-worth, and I revamped my individual coaching program to focus on burnout and imposter syndrome. I also started a group coaching program and a year-long mastermind group focused on somatic tools. I won a Woman Entrepreneur of the Year award, too—which was very meaningful to me because I was nominated by a client!

I could serve my clients with integrity and quality because I had the freedom of time and energy that was so important. **I was able to be a role model for them on how to feel energized, set boundaries, and prioritize themselves.**

How can you identify your visibility obstacles? Think of your mind like a super-smart computer that's always on even when you don't realize it. This part of your mind, called the subconscious, is like the background apps on your phone: it does a lot without you telling it to. This is important because this part of our brain keeps us alive and keeps us safe.

But that's why doing anything new or out of your comfort zone can be so hard. Your brain is like a programmable thermostat. You try to increase your capacity from 80 to 85, but it will click you back down to 80.

The subconscious mind is also like a big storage room for your memories. It keeps everything you've ever experienced—all your past events, what you thought about them, and the meaning you took from them. Our subconscious beliefs largely form before the age of seven because, during these early years, our brains are in a highly impressionable state, like sponges absorbing water and children are deeply influenced by their environments, experiences, and the behaviors and words of those around them, creating foundational beliefs and attitudes that can last a lifetime (Bruce Lipton, "The Shortform Book Guide to The Biology of Belief" [www.shortform.com/app/book/the-biology-of-belief]).

Seemingly simple phrases like "you are overreacting" from a parent can lead an individual to constantly question and invalidate their own feelings and reactions, pushing them to work harder to prove their worth or to suppress their visibility. "The subconscious beliefs and the resulting self-sabotage can sometimes serve as a protective mechanism, acting on an unconscious level to prevent us from experiencing perceived threats or discomforts" (Leonard Mlodinow, *Subliminal: How Your Subconscious Mind Rules Your Behavior* [New York: Pantheon Books, 2012]).

Did you know that 95% of your behavior is driven by your subconscious thoughts? But don't despair:

1. **Recent research on neuroplasticity is not just scientifically intriguing; it's also incredibly empowering.** It suggests that we have the ability to shape our own brains' development and function through the experiences we choose and the behaviors we reinforce. Knowing that our brains can adapt and change gives us a real basis for hope and motivation. Dr. Celeste Campbell writes, "[P]hysiological changes in the brain [. . .] happen as the result of our interactions with our environment. From the time the brain begins to develop in utero until the day we die, the connections among the cells in our brains reorganize in response to our changing needs. This dynamic

process allows us to learn from and adapt to different experiences" (Celeste Campbell, PsyD, "What Is Neuroplasticity?" Brainline.org, July 26, 2018 [https://www.brainline.org/author/celeste-campbell/qa/what-neuroplasticity]).

This idea is closely connected to how we build confidence. You might think you need to feel confident before you try something new, but it actually works the other way around. When you do something new, even if you're not feeling confident, your brain starts to change because of neuroplasticity. Each time you step out of your comfort zone and try, your brain adjusts, stores this new experience, and begins to understand that you can handle more than you thought. Over time, these experiences build up, and that's when you start feeling more confident. It's like exercising a muscle: the more you use it, the stronger it gets.

2. **Pay attention to fears that are holding you back.** Avoiding the limelight, whether by dodging speaking opportunities or sidestepping sales calls, is a sign you may have limiting beliefs that are stunting your growth. Look for other behaviors, such as not emailing your list to make offers because you are afraid to "bother" them. Catch yourself when you are procrastinating, trying to be perfect, or people-pleasing. These are all symptoms of underlying fear. **Exploring the potential hidden benefits of remaining unseen can reveal much about our fears.**

When you tune into your emotions and become aware of the "fight, flight, or freeze" stress responses, you open a door to understanding potential triggers in your life. By listening to these subtle cues, you empower yourself to grow, transform, and live a life filled with intention and inner peace.

Now What? Get Support

Nowadays, we have access to an incredible array of tools designed to uncover the beliefs that limit us and assist in transforming these beliefs. My approach involves equipping my clients with a diverse toolkit, enabling them to select the methods that resonate most strongly with them. While I maintain that affirmations alone aren't a comprehensive fix, I do believe they play a crucial role in initiating the brain's rewiring process. Utilizing present-tense affirmations such as "I am" statements can be particularly effective. However, to truly capitalize on their power, I believe it's essential to pair them with vivid visualization and emotional engagement. Imagine not only the act of speaking on a podcast but also the joy and pride of sharing that achievement with friends and family. It's this emotional connection that significantly amplifies the impact, guiding the brain toward genuine transformation.

I frequently supplement this work with two techniques that provide a unique lens through which to process and alter our beliefs:

- **Eye Movement Desensitization and Reprocessing (EMDR)** facilitates access to disturbing memories and sensations stored in the subconscious mind. Using bilateral stimulation, this technique aims to reduce the emotional impact and emotional charge such memories carry. It encourages the brain to reprocess these memories. A belief such as "I am powerless" stemming from a traumatic event can be transformed into "I am strong and in control."

- **Emotional Freedom Technique (EFT),** also known as "tapping," involves tapping on specific meridian points on the body while focusing on particular negative emotions and sensations as well as statements related to their experiences. The act of tapping on these meridian points is believed to send signals to the part of the brain that controls stress responses and the body's overall energy balance, according to traditional Chinese medicine. Regular EFT can help reduce cortisol levels and rewire the brain (S.Y. Gregory, "The benefits of EFT tapping and how to do it, according to therapists" [Livestrong.com, September 12, 2023, https://www.livestrong.com/article/13778317-eft-tapping]).

***

Success Story

My client Jenna had built her marketing business from the ground up. Yet, despite her passion and talent, her brand remained a well-kept secret. It wasn't the quality of her work that held her back but her fear. Jenna was terrified of criticism. I was able to pick up on her fear of being judged.

I introduced Jenna to Emotional Freedom Technique (EFT), or "tapping," explaining how it could help recalibrate her emotional response to visibility and being judged.

As Jenna tapped on each meridian point, I guided her to voice her fears: "Even though I'm terrified of being judged, I can learn to accept myself."

It was during our second session that we made a significant breakthrough. A harsh critique from a college professor had left her feeling exposed and unworthy. We focused our tapping on this pivotal moment, working to release its grip on her. Jenna started sharing her story and the inspiration behind her work on social media, each time feeling more comfortable and confident in the spotlight.

Her business began thriving, with features in local magazines and a growing online following. But more importantly, Jenna had found her voice!

***

Remember, you have a story to tell and solutions to offer. Remember your "why." **I am so proud of my program that I don't fear marketing it.** I know it has changed women's lives! The program transforms high-performing women who feel emotionally drained, physically exhausted, and constantly overwhelmed, and it offers a solution to go from overwhelm to vitality, clarity, and confidence.

Align your actions with your values. I love the way the program combines therapy's depth with the action-oriented focus of coaching. **Being myself, focusing on my strengths, and communicating my message in a manner that's authentic to me** allows me to concentrate on refining a select few strategies to excellence rather than spreading my efforts too thinly across multiple fronts. From there, my priority is to nurture genuine connections.

This balanced blend of authenticity, strategic focus, and unwavering belief in the transformative power of my program forms the cornerstone of my approach, making the task of marketing not just effortless but deeply rewarding.

Jenna's journey and mine were not just about business growth; they were about personal transformation. As I stepped into the light, becoming more visible, my reach extended, allowing my message to resonate with a wider audience and amplify the impact I sought to create. **This visibility brought in more clients, affording me the flexibility to avoid the pitfalls of burnout and sustain a healthier, more fulfilling path forward.**

Let my story be a reminder that your time is now! **It IS possible** to transform your beliefs and, consequently, your life. *Embrace your worth, step into visibility, and watch as the world opens up to the solutions only you can provide.*

You-First Visibility Tips

1. Neuroplasticity means that your current beliefs are not set in stone; they can be reshaped, redefined, and uplifted. By believing your inner experiences and challenges are your superpower instead of judging them, you will unlock a future where you feel proud and confident to be visible.

2. The world needs your gifts, and the only way to sustain a strong foundation from which you can be visible and give generously is to put yourself first. Nurture your own mind, body, and spirit, and replenish your energy regularly. This is what will truly give you the clarity you need to make the decisions that will lead to your visibility.

Mary Struzinsky, LCSW

Mary Struzinsky, LCSW, is an award-winning licensed clinician and celebrated somatic empowerment coach, boasting over three decades of clinical and management experience. Her expertise lies in empowering high-achieving, busy women, guiding them to uncover the hidden beliefs that deplete their energy and perpetuate a cycle of overthinking, over-functioning, and overworking. As the creator of the program Exhausted to Energized and Empowered, Mary takes an approach that is both compassionate and results-oriented, focusing on equipping women with the energy, confidence and TIME to lead lives that resonate deeply with their core values without guilt. Certified in both EMDR (Eye Movement Desensitization and Reprocessing) and EFT (Emotional Freedom Technique), Mary coaches in a way that transcends traditional methods. By honing in on the intricate connection between the brain and nervous system, she facilitates lasting change from within. It's not just about surface-level solutions; it's about rewiring the very fabric of one's being for sustained empowerment. Mary is the co-author of two books (*Visibility Today* and *Packaging Your Expertise*) and a compelling speaker, often sharing her poignant personal journey of burnout as a former executive director of a national human service agency.

Social Media Links

Email: marys@starcitycoaching.com
Phone: 540-815-0543
Website: https://www.starcitycoaching.com/
Facebook public pages: https://www.facebook.com/starcitycoaching
https://www.facebook.com/mary.struzinsky
Facebook group: https://www.facebook.com/groups/starcitycoaching
LinkedIn: https://www.linkedin.com/in/mary-struzinsky-lcsw/
X: https://x.com/marystru
YouTube: https://www.youtube.com/@marystruzinsky/
Medium: https://medium.com/@marygstru
IG: https://www.instagram.com/starcitycoaching/

Chapter 2
Create the Momentum
by Rebecca Hall Gruyter

As the words flowed from her fingertips, Emily felt a sense of satisfaction. Her creative genius shone through the pages, each sentence a carefully crafted gem. But as she put the finishing touches on her masterpiece, a sense of dread crept into her heart. She knew that releasing her book to the world was only the first step. The thought of facing the music was a daunting task that loomed large, threatening to overshadow the joy of her creation. She had poured her soul into the pages, and the prospect of promoting her book filled her with anxiety. Emily sighed, knowing that this was necessary. She had to step into the arena of marketing and self-promotion, a realm that seemed to demand a different kind of skill set, one that didn't come naturally to her. How would she find the time and energy to tackle this new challenge? Her mind raced as she considered the unfamiliar terrain ahead. Yet, she was determined.

Have you ever felt like Emily? You've written your book or created your program, and yet you feel stuck as to how to share your brilliance out into the world . . . how to create the momentum needed to drive engagement and activity. You have something special that you want to share with the world, but the marketing and promotional skills you need to do this are not in your skill set.

You are very creative and want to share your vision with the world. But there are those certain tasks that go along with marketing yourself that you just can't seem to find time for or don't have enough specific knowledge about. It is okay not to know everything. It's okay to get help.

Today, it's not enough to create something powerful. You also have to let people know about it. If they don't know it exists, then it won't be able to help them. You need to be willing to be the spokesperson for your creation. Plan to market and promote it prior to launch, during the initial release, and on an ongoing basis. Your marketing and promotion drive the traffic and sales—not the brilliance of your content.

When is it time to find help?

Your vision and what you want to share with the world is strong. But if you find that the thought of certain tasks to share that vision has you pausing, then don't pause! Find someone who can help you. If you find you are missing opportunities, calls, emails, interviews, and/or appointments, then it is time to get help. If you aren't sure how to create or grow a list, then it is time to get help. If you aren't sure how to use social media to create engagement and an ongoing promotional plan, then it is time to get help/support. You don't have to do it all yourself.

Putting your ideas out into the world can be daunting, but it doesn't have to be. Ask for help!

What types of things can you find help doing?

- Scheduling calls, appointments and interviews
- Social media promotional campaigns
- Growing your list
- Social media and content creation
- Email marketing and management
- Website design and updates
- Getting noticed on podcasts

So many brilliant experts, authors and leaders create wonderful books, powerful programs, and transformational content . . . but they get stuck by missing the opportunity to get help so that they can stay in their brilliance and drive traffic to all they are bringing forward. We don't have to do it all on our own or figure out everything. We can bring in brilliant and talented support to help us achieve all that we are looking to achieve and bring to the world.

"An intelligent person is one who knows his limitations." —Kamilla, "The Dating Boss"

Do you need help? It's time to get back to doing what you love and take those tasks off your plate that you don't feel comfortable doing!

As you get excited about the possibility of getting help and support, here are some keys to be clear on so that you are able to bring in the right support and help for you. The clearer you are on the following items, the more easily those you bring in to support you can align and help you achieve all you are looking to achieve.

Here are some tips to help you bring in the right support for you:

1. Be clear on who you are trying to reach and why.

2. Have a plan to promote before, during and after the release of your book or program. (If you don't have one yet, work with your team/support to create one.)

3. Where are you feeling stuck and needing support? This will help you identify and prioritize where you may need help first.

4. What do you want/like to do and what do you want to delegate to others?

5. Talk with an expert who has achieved what you are looking to achieve and see if they can help or refer you to someone who can help you with your needs and goals.

6. Put together a plan of action and steps for consistent promoting and marketing. This plan can be either for you to implement or for the person coming aboard to implement.

7. Implement the plan. Put it into action. And make sure to check in every few weeks (at least monthly) to see what can be tweaked or adjusted to further support you and your goals.

8. Celebrate the support and being willing to bring your gifts and talents to the world!

When you trust and ask for help, you can achieve so much! This made such a difference for me in my trajectory and growth. When I was willing to get support, bring in help, and delegate, I was able to grow more quickly and reach more people. I didn't have to figure out everything on my own; I could learn from others and trust others to help me get the message out. I could stay in my zone of genius while bringing in team members that had the skill set to reach more people, help with website tech issues, manage my email systems, and even help with social media marketing and promotion. I was able to grow my team step by step, over time, starting small with a few hours here and there until eventually we were able to create a team of over twenty people with a dynamic and powerful global reach. Now I have a company that has multiple facets designed to help people's dreams come true. Our company helps clients reach more people with their bestselling books and transformational messages by speaking on more stages/platforms and being positioned as the expert they are out in world . . . all while increasing their visibility.

What are you looking to do and bring forward? How could building your team and starting to delegate more with clear plans make a difference for you?

Here is what it did for Emily:

Emily's mind buzzed with the realization that marketing her work required skills she had yet to develop. She knew that seeking help was the sensible thing to do, but the prospect of explaining her needs to someone else made her feel vulnerable. However, the thought of letting her exquisite story go unnoticed due to her own shortcomings was too painful to bear. With determination and a hint of trepidation, she decided to seek assistance, knowing full well that her vision was too precious to risk failing.

She approached a seasoned writer, someone she admired for their expertise in the craft and their ability to connect with readers. Her heart raced as she shared her predicament, explaining that although she could create stories, she struggled with the business side of things. To her relief, the established writer smiled warmly and shared a similar experience from their past, assuring Emily that many creators face this dilemma. The seasoned writer offered to guide her through the maze of marketing and self-promotion. They outlined a strategy that involved harnessing the power of social media and crafting captivating snippets to tease and entice potential readers.

Together, they crafted a game plan that played to Emily's strengths and identified the areas where she needed further support. With renewed enthusiasm, Emily felt empowered to navigate the unfamiliar terrain ahead, knowing that she had an experienced guide by her side. Each new post, each interaction with potential readers was a learning experience, and soon the dread she once felt was replaced with excitement. She realized that sharing her vision could be a joyful experience, free from the anxiety that had once plagued her. She could reach the world with her message.

You can, too! You can create momentum by sharing out consistently and by getting support and help where you need it. Your brilliance, your creation, your book/program is needed in the world. Take the steps for it be easy for those who need it to discover it, find it, and lean into it. That is what marketing and promotion are about: making the information, book, program, or resource easy to find by those who need it most. Be willing get help in sharing out. Be willing to be seen, be heard, and SHINE!

Rebecca Hall Gruyter

Rebecca Hall Gruyter is a global influencer, a #1 international bestselling author, a compiler and publisher (helping over 1,000 authors become bestsellers), a radio show host (reaching over 1 million listeners on 8 networks), and an empowerment leader. She has built multiple platforms to help experts reach more people. These platforms include radio, podcasts, books, magazines, the Speaker Talent Search, and live events, creating a powerful promotional reach of over 10 million!

Rebecca is the CEO of RHG Media Productions, the founder of Your Purpose Driven Practice, and the creator of the Speaker Talent Search. Rebecca has personally contributed to 40+ published books and multiple magazines, and she has been quoted in major media including Huffington Post, ABC, CBS, NBC, Fox, and Thrive Global. Today, she wants you to be seen, be heard, and SHINE!

Email: Rebecca@YourPurposeDrivenPractice.com
Websites and Social Media:
http://www.YourPurposeDrivenPractice.com
http://www.RHGTVNetwork.com
http://www.SpeakerTalentSearch.com
https://www.facebook.com/rhallgruyter
https://www.linkedin.com/in/rebecca-hall-gruyter-2802669/
http://www.x.com/Rebeccahgruyter
https://www.instagram.com/rhg_global_community/
http://www.EmpoweringWomenTransformingLives.com
http://www.rebeccahallgruyter.linktoexpert.com/

Chapter 3
Business Magic with the *Energetic Feng Shui*™ System
by Deborah Wiener

Growing up in a life of poverty, abuse, and chaos meant it wasn't safe to be seen or heard. I made myself invisible, lost my voice and dissociated from the world to survive. Hypervigilance and hypersensitivity to people and energy around me became my mode of operation. This sensitivity led to the development of an acute sense of awareness of threats and danger and attuning to the energy around me. I spent many years healing, starting with talk therapy and evolving into energetic healing modalities that cleared the distorted programming, beliefs and imprints of my childhood. These distorted and limiting beliefs had blocked me from seeing new possibilities in life. This expanded my reality beyond anything I could have imagined. I now get to live a powerful and joy-filled life.

As is true for most empaths and highly sensitive people, I absorbed the energy of those around me and did not understand that this energy does not belong to me. This pattern led me to lose my identity and dissociate, and I lived a life that was filled with chaos, stress and anxiety. When we dissociate, we leave our body; therefore we are not present and cannot access our feelings. For decades, I was filled with everyone else's energy and feelings. I believed that it was my responsibility to save everyone, not only my family but everyone in the world. I became so outwardly focused that there was no room to develop a sense of self. Once this belief was identified, I learned how to clear the energy of others and create a protective energetic shield around myself. I learned the tools and practices that allowed me to master the art of observing, not absorbing, others' energy.

Childhood trauma also forced me to disconnect from my intuition. I have discovered that connecting to and learning to trust our intuition is essential to positive manifestation. Through numerous intuitive development classes (including studying Remote Viewing, a technique used by the CIA at the Monroe Institute!), I was able to reconnect with my intuition. This allowed me to be discerning and to make healthy choices by being aware of energy. As someone who has studied and experienced numerous healing modalities and practitioners, I would like to share a key piece of wisdom in your healing journey—develop and trust your intuition first and foremost! Ask yourself: How do I feel around this person, place or thing? Listen to your body; it speaks the language of your intuition. Be aware of how you feel, because all the answers are inside of you.

In addition to becoming a certified Western Feng Shui Master, I studied many nontraditional healing modalities over the last thirty-five years. My search for clarity, peace and healing led me to integrate and synthesize these teachings into a unique set of tools to assess, clear and transform energy. Western Feng Shui provided me with a foundation for creating spaces that allow solitude, peace and harmony to flow. I expanded this wisdom into my unique system of energy healing that transforms the energy within you and around you, creating beautiful spaces that you feel you never want to leave!

The Energetic Feng Shui System™ is my unique healing and manifestation system for working with energy to create positive change, attract and manifest anything you desire. The dogma and rigidity of most of the disciplines and modalities I studied felt restrictive and did not align with my intuition, my truth. Intuition is the foundation of *The Energetic Feng Shui System*™. You cannot create and manifest unless you are present, conscious, and connected to your intuition. It is your personal GPS system guiding you to peace, harmony and balance. It will never let you down.

Taking elements from traditional feng shui and adding elements from many more solution-oriented modalities and disciplines, I created *The Energetic Feng Shui System*™. This system is the culmination of my intuitive skills, business knowledge and energy alchemy skills.

Energy is everywhere and everything is energy. It is important that we are aware of the energy around us and within us. Your thoughts, words, and actions are the energy that create your reality. When you understand this concept, you become aware of how powerful you truly are. You are the creator of your reality. The only way to manifest is by raising your energetic frequency to match what you desire.

My multidimensional energy healing system combines elements from traditional feng shui, quantum physics, and Human Design and other success systems into a toolbox that creates exponential change. Ultimately, this cutting-edge system alchemizes energy to match like energy. This system taps into frequencies that activate expansiveness, where opportunities, dreams and wishes come true!

Allow me to illustrate the power of *The Energetic Feng Shui System*™ with a money example. Everything is energy, including money. A primary principle of *The Energetic Feng Shui System*™ is "Where Energy Flows, Money Goes™!" Money allows you to do the things you want in life. I used *The Energetic Feng Shui System*™ to support the creation of a profitable family business.

Thirty-five years ago, my husband started what is now a multi-million-dollar business, beginning in a garage with a well-worn Toyota truck (with a lien on it) and a $5,000 loan. While he was busy launching the business, I was deep in my study of the laws of energy. Partnering with him, I recognized that the business needed implementation of organized structures to allow the business and money to flow. As an energy detective, I identified areas of the business that needed positive improvement and change to create energetic flow. For example, a customized inventory management system replaced manual labor, catapulting the business to run with ease. The sales team and other key employees needed new leadership and development. We used my system to overhaul the hiring, training and compensation structures, leading to an A+ team. As the money began to flow, we paid back that $5,000 loan many times over, and our life trajectory changed.

Let's dig a little deeper into my process. The first pillar of *The Energetic Feng Shui System*™ addresses the space. Space could mean a building, an office, land, or a room. The process begins with assessment of the space and often includes cleaning and decluttering. Let me illustrate the value of this pillar with the story of Walter, the owner and operator of a local mechanic shop. Walter struggled to retain customers and employees. When you walked into the shop to check in, you wanted to run right out the door. The bathroom was filthy, the office was cluttered, and the energy was polarizing. His shop needed physical and energetic cleaning and clearing. Unfortunately, he wasn't open to change, and his business suffered because of it.

Thankfully, our family business was not resistant to change! On one of my visits, I saw that the office was accumulating dust and clutter (just like Walter's shop!) and the energy had become stagnant. I went into action mode and used the three components of feng shui to assess and clear the space, clean and declutter, and finally improve the placement of color and objects. The newly revamped office created a beautiful environment no one wanted to leave. This process transitions spaces from "Ugg, I don't like it here! I want to run right out the door!" to, "Ahh, I could stay here forever!" Over the next few years, these new systems, clean and updated space, and the investments in our employees allowed us to realize significant profits (even through a recession and the pandemic).

Here is another example of the power of this revolutionary system at work in the real world.

Recent chiropractic graduates Susan and Charles specialized in the National Upper Cervical Chiropractic Association (NUCCA) Method. Struggling to pay rent and student loans, Charles was a full-time student pursuing an advanced degree in chiropractic imaging. Susan worked part-time in a cramped chiropractic office with the owner, Mr. Crane. With one treatment room, she only saw clients from 7:00 to 9:00 am. Her few clients weren't allowed to talk because once Mr. Crane came in, talking would "disturb him." He marched in like the school headmaster, immediately restricting the energy. Clients were more stressed after treatments than before! Susan had few clients with little prospect for more. No business cards, no marketing, no one knew who she was! She couldn't bill clients' health insurance, which limited her client base.

That's where I stepped in. As I was doing a feng shui analysis of Susan's office, she shared with me that she wanted a space of her own where she could practice the NUCCA method of chiropractic care *and* start a family. She wondered,

"Can I have both?" I assured her that we could attract a perfect match; it was just waiting out there in the quantum field for the perfect match of energy. Remember, our thoughts, words and actions create our reality. We can all manifest the life and business of our dreams. When Susan verbalized her desires, she set in motion the first step in manifesting. That conversation activated my gift of connecting others to opportunities. My expertise in matching the energy of people's desires was set in motion!

Soon after, I was walking down the grocery aisle, and I ran into my friend Liz, who was noticeably upset. "Hi Liz, what's wrong?" She tearfully replied, "I am losing my job!" She adored the owners of a very successful chiropractor's office, where she had worked as a masseuse for many years. The business owners were retiring after thirty-five years in business, and they were moving to Arizona to be with their grandchildren. While Liz was happy for them, she was concerned that if they could not find a NUCCA Method chiropractor to buy the business, the business would shut down and she would be out of a job and have to start from scratch.

Susan and Charles came to mind immediately, and I reached out to them to share this amazing opportunity. "This could be the answer to your desires for a dream business and the opportunity to start a family!" Initially, Susan's limiting belief systems paralyzed her. She could not muster the courage to call the business owners. Like many people, when she was presented with a new possibility or reality, she could not acknowledge or recognize the opportunity. Belief systems such as "I am not worthy" and "This is too good to be true" or fears of failure or success show up and block us from moving forward.

When we are manifesting a new reality, it is essential to evaluate our belief systems. These limiting belief systems are unconscious; we are often not aware they even exist. The catalyst for change is transforming your energy, because energy matches like energy.

Susan decided to work with me to understand why she was resisting making the phone call. We discovered the issue came from a generational belief system about worthiness. After transmuting the belief system and transforming her energy into alignment to the opportunity, she had the courage and confidence to make that call to the owners. Once she took action, everything changed! All areas of her life, business and income improved. *The Energetic Feng Shui System*™ activates the energetic laws of attraction, magnetizing your dreams into reality.

Fast-forward to a few months later. Susan and Charles bought the business from the Shelbys, who were delighted to have them take over their practice! It was a match made in heaven! They bought a complete, well-established business with an experienced staff well-versed in billing insurance, state-of-the-art imaging equipment, a lobby filled with toys and books for their infant and pediatric clients, a nutritionist, an acupuncturist, and, of course, Liz as their masseuse. There was plenty of room to work with multiple clients.

Susan and Charles had a match made in heaven , but it wasn't quite heaven yet! Both pillars of my system were needed for a smooth transition. Even successful businesses need an Energetic Feng Shui™ clearing. Whenever someone leaves, energy is left behind. We started with Pillar 1 with cleared, clean and upgraded energy. Then we cleaned, organized, and strategically placed colors, including fresh new paint, plants, and crystals.

It was now time for Pillar 2: assess the office staff and practitioners to ensure they had the right people, in the right position, with the right compensation. A few of the staff needed to be replaced or reassigned. Under my guidance, they created their A+ team. We found two new NUCCA Method practitioners and an accomplished and trustworthy office manager to run the day-to-day operations of the company. Now the company's energy is flowing, and with their new team it seems like the business magically runs itself! This new staff allowed Susan to go on maternity leave and spend time with her baby. The dream she set in motion in her old office had finally manifested—she had her successful business *and* a family!

The Energetic Feng Shui System™ works! The energy that attracted Susan and Charles to me aligned with buying a successful business. It allowed them to pay off student loans, purchase their dream home and start their family! Their financial impact and influence in the community has grown exponentially. They have hundreds of loyal clients and more income than they imagined at this stage of their life! My energy magnetizes what my clients' desire; that's why they hire me!

When energy in a business is stagnant, sales become stagnant. If your business is not profitable, you have a hobby, not a business.

This unique system supports you in redesigning your life and business, opening doors to infinite opportunities and possibilities. Your visibility, influence and impact correlate to your energetic frequency. *The Energetic Feng Shui*

System™ magnifies, amplifies, and multiplies the vibrations and frequencies of the energies of your desires to new levels of consciousness where everything is possible.

When you implement *The Energetic Feng Shui System*™, challenges are overcome with creative solutions and you are led to the life of your dreams. The visibility, impact and influence of energetic flow are limitless. Remember, "Where Energy Flows, Money Goes™!"

Deborah Wiener

Deborah Wiener is an international bestselling author, international award-winning speaker and distinguished Toastmaster. She is a columnist for *RHG Digital Magazine* and has been featured on numerous radio shows, TV shows, podcasts, and internet TV shows.

Deborah is a lifelong learner and dedicated practitioner of energy. She is a certified Western Feng Shui Master and a Reiki Master. She is a shaman and practices quantum physics and various healing modalities, including Human Design, Enneagram, Spiritual Response Technique (SRT), Sound Healing, and many more!

She is a co-owner of QuickScrews/QuickBolt International Corporation, a multi-million-dollar family-owned importing business of over thirty-six years. Deborah created her own change management system and manifestation methodology, *The Energetic Feng Shui System*™. This cutting-edge system increased revenues during a recession and the pandemic!

This more complete transformational system activates energy by synthesizing teachings from traditional feng shui, quantum physics, and Human Design and other success systems. This interdisciplinary system supports you to redesign your life and business, enabling more expansion and success. The difference between traditional feng shui and *The Energetic Feng Shui*™ *System* is the magnitude of results.

Deborah Wiener is an expert who converts problems into solutions and dreams into reality!

Contact Info and Social Media Links:

Email: dwiener30@gmail.com
Phone: 001-925-580-0350
Website: www.deborahwiener.com
Facebook: https://www.facebook.com/deborah.l.wiener
LinkedIn: https://www.linkedin.com/in/deborah-wiener-b6009b167/
YouTube: https://www.youtube.com/channel/UCean6OtIAhs44jLJy9v1izA
Instagram: https://www.instagram.com/fengshuibusinessconsultant/

SECTION 2:

Chapter 4
Amplifying Authentic Voices: The Power of Video in Building Personal Branding
by Maureen Ryan Blake

My journey is a remarkable tale of resilience, self-discovery, and empowerment, deeply rooted in my origins from Brooklyn—a place that has undoubtedly shaped the resilient spirit I carry with me today. My story isn't just about the places I've lived, from Florida to Chicago, Colorado, San Diego, and now Little Rock, but about the profound personal evolution I've experienced along the way.

Living with the challenge of becoming deaf in my late twenties, I faced more than just the physical loss of hearing; it was also a profound loss of my voice and confidence. As someone who loved to sing and dreamed of becoming a rock star, the silence was not just an absence of sound but the shattering of a dream, a silence in my soul. This wasn't just a journey through different landscapes, but a deep internal struggle and transformation. Initially, I attributed the loss of my voice to the constant moves, the change of environments. But it was so much more. It was about finding silence and then finding sound again in new ways.

In Little Rock, surrounded by my nineteen ducks and five dogs, I've found more than just a home. I've found a sanctuary where I began to reclaim what was lost. This wasn't just about adapting to hearing loss but about rediscovering my voice through new modes of expression and connection. My journey has been about tapping into my innate resilience and recognizing that my voice, though it may have changed, still holds power and influence.

I've dedicated the last five years not only to personal recovery and empowerment but also to helping others find and amplify their voices. Through my own experiences, I've become a beacon for others, exemplifying that even through significant challenges like deafness, relocation, and personal upheaval, one can emerge stronger and more determined.

My story is not just about overcoming but about thriving and inspiring. It's about how every challenge I've faced has been a step towards greater self-realization and how I've turned my trials into opportunities for growth, both for myself and for those I reach out to. As I continue on this path, I remember that my journey is one of continuous transformation—one where each day brings a new chance to be heard, to influence, and to inspire.

In our rapidly evolving digital age, visibility has become the linchpin of success. Whether you're an entrepreneur, a coach, or a content creator, establishing a commanding online presence is paramount for connecting with your audience and making a lasting impact. This chapter will delve into the transformative power of video in sculpting personal branding and amplifying authentic voices. With insights from the innovative approaches I developed through my marketing social media marketing company Maureen Ryan Blake Media, we will explore the strategies and techniques essential for navigating the complex journey to visibility in the digital landscape.

Unleashing Authenticity Through Video Content

In the vibrant arena of our digital world, authenticity is not merely a key to success—it's the very core of substantial personal branding. When we embrace authenticity, we commit to our true selves, sharing genuine experiences and forging deep, meaningful connections. Video content emerges as a potent medium that enables us to vividly express our authentic selves and engage with our audience in impactful ways.

Utilizing video allows us to present our personality, values, and expertise, thereby building a robust emotional connection with our viewers. This connection transcends mere benefit; it is fundamental for cultivating trust, fostering loyalty, and setting ourselves apart in the densely populated digital landscape. Authenticity in video content is not about portraying perfection—it's about showcasing relatability, allowing people to see the real you, flaws and all, making your brand both relatable and memorable.

In this chapter, I will guide you through the nuances of creating video content that resonates authentically. We'll explore strategies to ensure you remain true to your core while forging a real connection with your audience. We'll discuss integrating personal stories into your videos, transforming each segment from merely informative to deeply personal and engaging. By the end, you will appreciate how to utilize video not just as a tool for communication but as a vibrant canvas for your personal expression. Let's embark on this journey to ensure your personal brand is not only seen but truly felt.

Creating authentic video content demands an intimate understanding of your brand identity and messaging. It involves being transparent, vulnerable, and genuinely relatable to viewers. Authenticity in video content is not about achieving perfection but about being real and authentic. Sharing personal stories, insights, and experiences helps build trust and credibility with your audience, laying a solid foundation for your personal brand.

Moreover, authenticity is not merely a one-time act but a continuous commitment to remaining true to oneself and consistently delivering value to your audience. It is about transparent communication, genuine interactions, and authentic storytelling. By embracing authenticity in your video content, you can distinguish yourself in a crowded digital environment and cultivate a loyal following of engaged viewers.

Crafting Compelling Narratives: The Art of Storytelling

Storytelling transcends being a mere skill—it is an art that captures hearts and minds, weaving messages into memorable experiences. Through storytelling, we foster emotional connections, evoke empathy, and inspire our audience to action. Video content serves as an especially dynamic medium for this art, enabling us to animate our narratives with compelling visuals, evocative music, and impactful narration.

Mastering storytelling in video requires constructing well-structured narratives that intrigue and engage. We infuse our stories with elements such as conflict and resolution, enriching them with profound character development. This method enables us to create narratives that deeply resonate, whether they're personal anecdotes, client testimonials, or the origins of a brand.

The power of storytelling goes beyond video; it transforms video content from simple information to relatable, engaging experiences that captivate viewers. By adopting storytelling techniques, you do more than share information; you invite your audience into a world you've crafted, offering them a place at your fireside.

It is important to lay the foundation for captivating stories, building tension and interest, and concluding in a manner that leaves your audience moved and motivated. Whether sharing personal journeys, highlighting customer successes, or unveiling your brand's genesis, learn to do so with a storyteller's flair—making your video content not only visible but profoundly impactful. The transformative power of storytelling helps to elevate your videos from the ordinary to the extraordinary.

Content Distribution and Engagement

Content distribution and engagement aren't just about broadening your reach—they're about making meaningful connections that resonate deeply with those who watch your videos. You want to develop techniques designed to foster viewer interaction that goes beyond mere views and likes. You want to build a vibrant community around your brand, one viewer at a time. It's about creating a space where your audience feels valued and engaged, encouraging them to not only consume your content but to become active participants in your narrative.

You can use the power of interactive elements like polls, live discussions, and Q&A sessions to transform passive viewers into active community members. These tools invite your audience into a two-way conversation, making them feel like part of your brand's journey and development. By engaging your viewers on this level, you not only increase their loyalty but also gain invaluable insights into their preferences and feedback, which can steer the direction of your future content.

Remember that each video you create is an opportunity to reinforce your brand's values and vision. Use your content to tell stories that inspire, educate, and resonate. Show your audience that behind every video is a passionate creator who cares deeply about bringing value and inspiration into their lives. Let's harness the full potential of your video content to build a lasting legacy and a community that grows stronger with every upload.

This journey isn't just about reaching a wider audience—it's about touching lives and making an impact. With each step, you're not only enhancing your brand's digital presence but also empowering others to connect with your authentic voice. So, let's continue to push boundaries and elevate your video strategy to new heights. Transform your digital landscape into a thriving ecosystem of engaged viewers and passionate advocates for your brand.

MONETIZATION

Monetize your passion. How does audience engagement enhance your revenue streams? As a passionate creator, your authenticity doesn't just resonate in your content; it's also a crucial element in your monetization strategy. Engaging with your audience on a personal level can transform viewers into patrons who are eager to support you, not just with their attention but financially as well.

Incorporating direct feedback mechanisms into your content, such as interactive polls or Q&A sessions, not only boosts engagement but also gives you invaluable insights into what your audience truly values. This two-way communication fosters a sense of community and belonging, making your viewers feel like they are a part of your creative process. When your audience feels valued, they are more likely to invest in your merchandise or memberships, seeing these purchases as extensions of their support for your journey.

Moreover, consider hosting live video sessions where you can interact with your audience in real time. These sessions can be pivotal in building a personal connection, sharing your gratitude, and discussing your products or membership benefits directly. The authenticity of live interactions often translates into increased trust and loyalty, which are essential for a sustainable monetization strategy.

As you develop these relationships, always remember to stay true to your values and the core message of your brand. Your integrity is your strongest asset, and maintaining it is key to a long-lasting and fruitful relationship with your audience. By balancing strategic monetization with heartfelt engagement, you create a powerful synergy that propels both your financial goals and your personal mission forward.

Harness the unique opportunities that video content provides, transforming your passion into a viable, thriving enterprise. Explore innovative ways to generate revenue while maintaining the integrity and authenticity that your audience has grown to love. Step confidently into this next phase, empowered by the knowledge that you can successfully monetize your passion without compromising the essence of what makes your brand truly special.

Harnessing Analytics for Strategic Success

It is important to understand the power of data in shaping your digital narrative. View your analytics not merely as numbers or charts but as a window into the hearts and minds of your audience. This perspective shift is crucial; it transforms analytics from intimidating figures into valuable allies on your creative journey. Look at trends in viewer behavior, dissect peak engagement times, and analyze audience demographics. This deep dive into analytics enables us to tailor content more precisely, ensuring it strikes a chord every time it reaches an audience member.

Additionally, you can harness these analytics to experiment with new content forms and distribution strategies, always testing and learning from the outcomes. This iterative process isn't just about improvement—it's about revolutionizing how you connect with your audience, making every interaction count.

By mastering these analytics tools, you'll not only keep your content dynamic and engaging but also stay ahead of industry trends, setting the pace rather than keeping up. This proactive stance is empowering: it assures that your content strategy is as vibrant and evolving as the digital landscape itself. Step into this analytics-rich world with confidence, knowing that every piece of data empowers you to create content that is ever more impactful, aligned, and resonant with your audience. Let's embrace these tools, turning analytics into one of the most powerful elements of your content creation arsenal.

Learning From the Best

Be willing to learn from others. See what others have discovered works or doesn't work as successful content creators create and serve their niche and followers. Blend their proven techniques with your unique style and vision. It's about crafting a brand that is authentically yours while standing on the shoulders of giants. Let their stories and wisdom ignite a fire within you to pursue excellence with unwavering dedication and to engage with your craft in ways that resonate sincerity and drive. Harness this knowledge and use it to sculpt a narrative that not only reaches but profoundly touches your audience, fostering a community that values and trusts your voice. As you learn from the best, you too will inspire others, continuing the cycle of innovation and influence in the vibrant world of video content.

Central to our discussion here is the ethical dimension of content creation. I believe we have a responsibility as creators to manage sensitive content with integrity and compassion. Your approach to content can profoundly impact your audience and shape the perception of your brand.

Additionally, it's important to stay abreast of the latest trends and platform updates. In the swiftly evolving digital landscape, being informed is not just beneficial—it's essential. Keeping your finger on the pulse of new developments ensures that your content remains fresh, relevant, and ahead of the curve.

My intention for writing this chapter is to arm you with a holistic perspective that helps you not only build a standout personal brand but also create deep, meaningful connections with your audience. May you craft your own unique narrative in the world of video content and shine!

HERE ARE MY VIDEO TIPS TO HELP YOU SHINE:

Let your true self shine. Nothing connects more deeply than being genuine. Embrace your unique qualities and let them shine through in your videos.

Connect with your viewers. Get to know who you're talking to. Tailoring your content to match your audience's interests will make your videos more engaging and meaningful.

Brighten your space. Good lighting can really uplift your video's quality. Whether it's a sunny window or a soft ring light, make sure your videos are well lit to show your best side.

Keep it snappy. Value your viewers' time by keeping your videos concise and packed with useful information. This keeps their attention and respects their busy schedules.

Clear audio is key. Invest in a good microphone to make sure every word you say is heard clearly, minimizing any distracting background noises.

Be confident and comfortable. Practice makes perfect. The more you rehearse, the more relaxed you'll appear on camera. Remember, your body language speaks volumes!

Share your stories. Everyone loves a good story. Share yours or highlight stories from others to add a personal touch that viewers can relate to.

Guide your viewers. Always include a friendly call to action at the end of your videos. Encourage viewers to engage further with your content in a welcoming way.

Polish your videos. A little editing can go a long way. Clean up your videos to keep them dynamic and interesting, adding elements that draw the viewer in.

Embrace growth and feedback. Stay curious and open to new ideas. The digital world is always evolving, and there's always something new to learn that can enhance your videos.

By embracing these tips, you'll not only improve the quality of your videos, but you'll also create a genuine connection with your audience. Remember, each video is a chance to let your unique light shine and to make a lasting impact. Stay open, keep learning, and keep sharing—your voice has the power to inspire!

Maureen Ryan Blake

Maureen Ryan Blake is a dynamic force in brand storytelling, renowned for her ability to bring compelling narratives to life. With a career that began on Wall Street with industry giants like Cantor Fitzgerald and NewsCorp, Maureen quickly distinguished herself through her keen insights and strategic vision.

Maureen has interviewed 200+ bestselling authors, inspirational leaders, thought makers, and captains of industry, always with a focus on allowing their true, authentic selves to shine. As an international bestselling author, content creator, and the founder of the boutique social media firm Maureen Ryan Blake Media, she has a proven track record of helping companies craft distinctive brand voices that resonate in the marketplace.

Maureen Ryan Blake Media specializes in executive interviews and video content production, offering tailored solutions that elevate brands and amplify their presence on social media. In her weekly podcast, she features thought leaders and inspirational figures, and she masterfully highlights their messages and stories. This ability to make others shine is her superpower, setting her apart in the crowded field of brand storytelling.

As a serial entrepreneur, Maureen has created several successful businesses and continues to support fellow entrepreneurs with genuine care and gratitude. Her mission is clear: to ensure every company's story is not only heard but also remembered. Her dedication to excellence and passion for storytelling make her an invaluable asset to brands wanting to make a lasting impact. Maureen's unwavering commitment to helping others shine through their authentic stories fuels her success and continues to inspire and empower everyone she works with.

Social Media

https://www.youtube.com/c/MaureenRyanBlakeMediaProduction
https://www.facebook.com/MRBMediaProduction
https://www.instagram.com/maureenryanblakemedia/
https://www.linkedin.com/in/maureen-ryan-blake/
https://www.twitch.tv/maureensduckworld

Chapter 5
Actionable Advice to Improve Your Online Visibility
by Mike O'Connor

I was quick to jump at the opportunity to be a part of this book due to the visibility that it could bring me and the Service Professionals Network (SPN).

My goal is to provide real information about visibility that inspires both thought and action without sounding like I'm selling you on the value of SPN. I want to help you see and bypass some of the hurdles that can overwhelm and block people from finding success. If I can provide some actionable information that helps you become more visible and successful, I have achieved my goals here.

I'll be sharing some thoughts on how to become more visible in the search engines, how to pick the best social media channels for your brand, and how to take things in stride while pushing for success.

Visibility often determines success or failure for any entrepreneur or business.

Becoming visible, and trustworthy, has been an important step toward finding success for people since the beginning of recorded history. Caesar made history, in part because he understood the importance of being more visible and better at public relations than his enemies. Much of what we know about the ancient world today is due to propaganda Caesar spread through his writings about his conquest of Gaul, the "Commentarii de Bello Gallico" (https://en.wikipedia.org/wiki/Commentarii_de_Bello_Gallico).

We may not be out conquering the world, but most small business owners still make a lot of sacrifices and take a lot of risks before they even open their doors. Many things have changed since the days of Caesar; the need to be visible and trusted by the general public has not.

It's still a dog-eat-dog world in a lot of ways, so trust is as hard to come by as visibility. Therefore, it makes sense for any business owner to have a basic understanding of how to make their business more visible, trusted, and appreciated by their customer base.

Brand visibility and recognition have a lot to do with consumer behavior. Consumers are much more likely to buy from brands that they are familiar with. Seeing and hearing about your products and services over and over again through advertisements, social media, word of mouth, and online search results leads to consumer recognition. People don't even really need to hear about your products and services as much as they need to see your business name and logo on a consistent basis.

Getting people to recognize your business name and logo in a positive way should be one of the big goals in any online marketing attempt. Making sales is always the top goal, but that doesn't happen often without brand recognition.

In this chapter, I will share some tips on how to make your business more visible online so you can reach more potential customers. I will also share some personal thoughts on how to stay somewhat sane while doing it.

1. Focus on Visibility as Much as You Do Ability.

Many people think you just have to put up a good website so people can find your business and buy your products or services. However, anyone that has opened an online store knows that isn't the case.

In a perfect world, the business with the best ability to deliver a quality service or product would be the one most consumers use. However, we do not live in a perfect world, so most consumers make their buying decisions based on popularity more than ability.

It doesn't matter how good your products or services are if no one knows or talks about them. A lot of small business owners get into business because they love what they do. They love the services they perform and products that they make. Many small business owners get into business because they want to make money doing what they like to do.

Successful small business owners understand that they have to put daily effort into marketing and branding the business, whether they like to or not. They also understand the best form of advertising is word of mouth and reputation.

Getting other people to talk about what you did for them in their time of need is the best way to increase visibility and earn more business. Social media and major search engines have even taken word-of-mouth branding opportunities to another level.

Now, one person's comments about your product or service can be seen by millions of people. Anything people post about your business is also out there forever, so it is what we call evergreen marketing. Reviews are always easy to find online, so they can be the best free marketing in the world.

2. Maximize Your Visibility by Asking for Reviews and Testimonials.

Most small business owners fail to understand the true value of earning online reviews from customers and colleagues. Don't be one of those small business owners. You should be asking every customer or professional colleague, many times, to leave you online feedback anywhere they can.

Reviews are beneficial in many ways. Even bad online reviews can drive traffic and have a positive impact. How you respond to bad reviews can make a big difference in how people see your business.

Whether you own or manage a small mom-and-pop restaurant, a home improvement company, a barbershop, or any other business, your customers are likely to look you up online. Customers are getting smarter all the time, so they're more than likely going to see what other people have to say about your products or services before making a buying decision.

Potential customers can also find your online reviews while searching for feedback on your competitors. Look at online reviews and professional testimonials as part of your sales funnel. A bigger funnel improves your chances of making a sale.

When your customers or colleagues leave you a business review or testimonial, they also merge your spheres of influence a bit. People who are connected to the people leaving you reviews or testimonials are likely to see that feedback at some point. People in their local area or industry, whether they are connected or not, are also more likely to see that feedback.

The longer and more descriptive reviews and testimonials will probably be seen and valued more by other consumers.

3. Don't stress over getting bad reviews.

In today's world, with today's consumers, receiving a bad online review isn't the end of the world. Consumers are smart and read between the lines. A business owner responding in a positive way to a less-than-positive review can often drive a lot of business. People don't expect businesses to be perfect, so business owner responses can turn a negative into a positive for the business.

People expect businesses that actually do business to have some less-than-perfect customer reviews. Taking ownership of mistakes and accountability when your business could have done better can attract a lot of customers. Handling unfair objections with reasonable explanations of what happened can also lead to a lot of opportunities, so don't fear getting bad reviews. Just handle them accordingly.

4. Online reviews drive traffic and sales.

People buy from businesses and brands that they know and trust. If consumers don't personally know about your business, they're most likely going to check for online reviews to see the good, the bad, and the ugly.

Online reviews and testimonials provide social proof about the value of or issues with any product or service. They also drive traffic and influence buyers more than anything else in today's digital world.

Major search engines love to provide people with the opportunity to leave online reviews and testimonials, because that is what people are looking for when making buying decisions. This social feedback also plays a big role in determining where your site pops up in the major search engines. Websites and businesses with online reviews are much more likely to be seen. They are also more likely to make the sale.

This is why it is very important for any business to strive to earn as much real online feedback from customers and colleagues as possible. Ask people to leave feedback wherever they can. Major search engines like to give people as much good information as possible. Therefore, they will show every bit of feedback they can about your business when consumers are searching for it.

5. Leverage social media to build your business.

There are many ways you can leverage social media to build your business. Each social media channel brings different opportunities. Some social media channels are better than others depending on what you're selling and how you're trying to sell it.

Research each social media channel a little bit to find the best way to market your business for you. Social media can drive business owners crazy if they let it. Set your social media time and efforts accordingly. If social media really drives you crazy, get someone else to do the posting and engaging, because someone needs to do it in today's business world. Don't ignore social media for any reason.

Social media is one of the most powerful tools any business owner or marketing agency can use to build a brand. Many people think the value of social media lies in the potential to reach an overwhelming amount of people with one piece of quality content. They're not wrong, but social media can also provide a lot of opportunities for businesses and brands that remain consistent without the viral reactions. It is very easy for any business owner to get frustrated with lack of instant results on social media, but you have to remember that brand recognition doesn't usually happen overnight.

6. ENGAGE AND SHARE QUALITY SOCIAL MEDIA CONTENT CONSISTENTLY.

Every business owner should want to put out quality social media content on a consistent basis. Creating engaging and shareable content can change fortunes for any brand in a hurry.

However, consistency in social media posting and activity is often underrated by most small business owners. Engaging with other peoples' social media content is also extremely underrated by most small business owners. Responding to other peoples' social media posts is a great way to expose your business page to their audience.

Now, what you should consider quality content and appropriate in regard to consistency will change a bit depending on the industry. A company that sells specific items for specific occasions probably shouldn't post as often as the local restaurants and nightlife venues.

Consistent posting, responding to engagement, and using relevant hashtags are great ways for any small business to grow through social media. Using the right hashtags is vital to success in local marketing campaigns. Tag your local areas, products, and services.

Share pictures of your business reviews and professional testimonials on social media. Ask the people that left the review if you can tag them in the social media post as a way of saying thank you for the review. Tagging other people or businesses in your social media posts helps invite their followers and connections to your page. It also helps introduce them to your audience, so it is great for online networking and visibility.

Research your competitors on social media. Look for what they're doing right and see what they're doing wrong. Get ideas from social media influencers outside your industry, too. Spend time researching what is working and not working inside and outside of your industry.

Offering discounts and special promotions to your followers on social media is a great way to build followers and sales. Ask people to show you that they're following your business on social media to get a discount. Don't be afraid to send someone coupons for the next purchase if they share your social media post. Simple strategies on social media are often the best.

7. PUT SOME THOUGHT INTO YOUR SOCIAL MEDIA BIOS.

Most social media channels provide an area where you can briefly describe your social media page and include links to your site. This is a big piece of social media marketing that many business owners miss.

If you make a good social media bio, you can drive traffic to your website by posting engaging content that doesn't even have much to do with your business. I have driven millions of clicks to the Service Professionals Network through social media bio links by posting nothing but silly memes.

The bio sections are probably the most important part of any social media channel for any business for a couple of reasons. People look at the bios, and a great bio can inspire a lot of clicks. Bio sections are also searchable on social media channels, so the right keywords can put your products and services right in front of people searching for them.

If your social media content is your bait, think of the social media bio as the hook. Your content should attract people to your bio, and your bio should push them to make a click to your site.

Search online for the best way to write a bio on any social media channel to find a bunch of great advice. There will be a lot of conflicting advice, because there is always more than one way to do things. A little research here and make a big difference in your ROI from social media marketing.

Don't be afraid to test out different bios. I change my social media bios frequently to keep up with what I am focusing on at the time.

8. Maintain and improve your brand visibility over time.

Remember that change is the only constant in this world, especially when it comes to maintaining and building a brand. Being consistent in your posting and messaging is important to building a strong brand that people can trust. That doesn't mean you should stick with strategies that aren't working. Don't be afraid to adjust your message or rebrand your business as necessary to stay relevant and ahead of the competition. A rebrand can be as simple as a new logo or as complex as a complete overhaul of your marketing strategy.

To successfully build your brand, you need to think about your strategy and goals a lot. Your strategy should be a long-term plan that requires time, creativity, and whatever resources you can dedicate to marketing. Your strategy should change accordingly depending on resources and other limits you may be facing. Online marketing is often the first thing that business owners cut out, but that never helps the business. No matter what is going on in your business, you have to make time and put effort into marketing on a consistent basis.

Your marketing strategy should deliver unique and positive ways to tell people about your products or services. If you can convey the purpose of your products or services while explaining how they can help people, you will begin to make some progress. If you can touch on the emotions of consumers, then you are more likely to turn a maybe into a sale.

When you think about branding, think about showing the personality and core values of your business. Personality can be really beneficial for building relationships and brands. The personality of your business should be something your customer base relates to.

9. Have fun, because that is how you shine brightest.

Every small business owner faces many challenging things every single day, so have fun with the marketing part. When you have fun, you become more creative and attractive to other people. People like fun, and there are plenty of other things about being in business that aren't necessarily fun.

Nothing good happens when you stress over things like social media or online marketing. Know that marketing online opens you up to the world, which includes a lot of unhappy people. Smiling is contagious, and I realize that negative comments generally come from unhappy people. Don't let other peoples' negativity affect your happiness or take away from your goals.

The Service Professionals Network (SPN) is something that I built to help connect people and businesses around the world. I also built it to have fun while shining as bright as I can in hopes of inspiring others to do the same. My journey has never been easy, but I've never struggled with getting attention. When you know how the internet works, you can become pretty visible in a short amount of time. Apply these tips consistently for a little while, and visibility will not be much of a concern.

Mike O'Connor

Mike O'Connor is the owner and creator of the Service Professionals Network (SPN). SPN is a social network for professionals looking to connect with more people, including local customers. With over 100,000 members and millions of monthly views, SPN is one the biggest online chamber of commerce networks in the world.

Facebook: https://www.facebook.com/SPNlocal
X: https://x.com/chicagomold1
Website: https://www.ServiceProfessionalsNetwork.com

Chapter 6
Interview Like a Pro
by Rebecca Hall Gruyter

> " People will forget what you said, people will forget what you did, but people will never forget how you made them feel." —attributed to Maya Angelou

The most impactful and personally rewarding strategy you can invest in to increase your visibility is simply to allow people to see you, hear you, feel you and learn from you. I have seen hundreds of expert, heart-centered entrepreneurs grow their businesses through speaking. My favorite way to reach out and make an impact on a lot of people (and a great way to break into speaking on stage) is to be a guest expert. When you are interviewed on a show or podcast, you are instantly positioned as a go-to expert in your field.

From hosting, producing and leading multiple weekly online radio/TV shows a week over the past ten years, I have found that most people don't know how show up effectively to really share and shine as a guest expert.

There are so many podcast and virtual interview opportunities that are now available . . . it provides a powerful opportunity for experts to share their gifts and message. There are more shows and opportunities that experts can have easy access to than in years past. Yet, with all this opportunity, I find most experts don't have a plan of what to do before, during or after their appearance. They become really busy at times with interviews . . . but haven't really been able to harness them to grow their list, reach the people they want to reach, and really, fully leverage each interview appearance. This means they are missing opportunities . . . working harder . . . and reaching fewer people. They aren't fully leveraging all the amazing content they are creating and the visibility opportunities that they could have . . . if only they had a plan. Your time, energy, gifts and talents are important. I want to help you be strategic in how you spend them so you can truly harness the visibility you are leaning into by choosing to share your message/information through interviews.

To support you in developing a plan to position you and your message, I share my show-tested top seven tips to be your absolute best and leverage the opportunity of being a guest expert interviewed on a radio show, podcast, summit, or other show format.

I'm going to share with you tips that will help you on a live interview show; however, you'll find these insights will be valuable whenever you speak in public. There is an art to showing up really well, like a pro. Learning these tips and putting them into practice will not only help you show up powerfully and like the pro you are . . . but also make you a great guest that hosts will want to ask back again and again.

Pro Tip #1: Prepare what you want to share with your viewers/listeners.

It's easy to feel nervous and, in the moment, forget even the most familiar information! Preparing ahead what you want to share will help you focus and not leave out anything important to you.

Write your ideas down in chunks that you can share in 90 seconds or less. Order them into bullet points that will help you remember the main points during the interview. You could also make a list of questions you would like to be asked (the host may ask you to submit some, so you'll be ready). This is a good way to condense your ideas into questions and then answer them with your "sound bites."

Don't memorize! This is a live interview, a conversation—not a presentation. You want to be flexible so that you can respond to your host without feeling stuck in your script.

Just before a show (or any public appearance you make), take a moment to ground yourself and breathe. Then listen and feel into whether there's anything more to add to the list that you are called to share today. Trust the answer you receive. Remember that you are in service to the people who are watching/listening to you. How you make them feel is more important than the exact words you say.

Pro Tip #2: Less is more.

The biggest mistake I see is a guest who talks too much! They get so excited about sharing that they get caught up and forget who's listening/watching. Time moves much faster than you think!

During your interview, make your responses in those sound bites of 90 seconds or less. Why is this important?

- You want the energy to change throughout the show, so you can keep your audience engaged, informed and entertained. You don't want them to get lost or lose interest in a long, rambling answer.

- You make the greatest impact if you can describe your points succinctly. It's a good practice whenever you talk about your work to be brief.

- Your host has a format and a schedule to follow. For example, there may be ad breaks in the show that have to be honored. Remember that this is the host's show. Allow them room to lead and to take breaks as needed to honor their show format.

Pro Tip #3: Be respectful of the host's space.

You are on their show as their guest. Act as if you were a guest in their home.

You might not realize what it's like for them on their side of the desk. Often there are a lot of moving parts they are managing: preparing their intros, timing the segments, taking calls or comments in chat, dealing with tech or engineering, managing the conversation with an eye for the flow of the show, managing countdowns to commercials, and bringing the show to a close successfully, to name just a few potential host distractions.

<u>Be a mindful/thoughtful guest</u>:

- Remember that even an experienced host may also be nervous. Be respectful of their space.

- Listen carefully to the question; don't interrupt or talk over the host.

- Allow them to run the conversation. Share your piece, then hand the ball back to them.

- If you think they are repeating a question, sometimes they just want you to go deeper. Just say, "Here's what I would like to add," and expand your answer.

- Don't use the phrase "May I add one more thing?" and then continue talking. Listen for their answer and be open to their saying no—remember, they are managing the time for the show.

- Extend grace to the host as they hold space for you, their listeners/viewers, and everyone and everything else that's involved in producing the event.

Pro Tip #4: Prepare yourself for success.

When you are invited to be interviewed, whether it's on a show, on stage, or any in-person format, do these things:

- Become familiar with the host—look at their website and social media presence.

- Listen to one or two shows prior to your interview date, so you get a feel for the flow.

- Prepare an introduction for the host, with the parts of your bio that fit the show. Remember that on-air time is precious, so keep it succinct!

- Ask your questions ahead of time, not an hour prior to the show . . . or as the show is just starting. A week in advance is great timing. Your questions might include: Am I able to make an offer? Share a link? If yes, what do you need me to provide you?

- Ask what information they want from you ahead of time. If they want questions, provide them. Honor their structure and flow.

- Always have a free gift available (make sure the host is okay with you sharing one) with a URL that is easy to read on air. Set up the web page so that when people sign up for your free gift, they are added to your email list. This is a great way to expand your reach, serve the listening audience, and grow your list.

PRO TIP #5: BE AWARE AND INTENTIONAL ABOUT HOW YOU ARE SPEAKING.

Most of us speak very fast when we're talking among friends. When you speak in public, slow your pace down a little bit. Your audience needs time to absorb the important things you are saying, to feel into it and lean in for more. So speak clearly and slowly, and let what you say land.

If a glitch or distraction happens during the interview, it's okay to pause. Just take a breath, relax and move on. You'll be fine—because you trust you are the expert, you know the information, and you are prepared.

Show up professionally and sit up attentively even if the show is not videotaped. This helps you keep your energy up and support your voice. Use the range of your voice to keep your audience engaged—this is something you can practice at home by just recording your voice on your phone, then listening for ways to sound strong and engaging.

Pro Tip #6: Build in promoting the show before and after the interview.

Many guests make the mistake of thinking the main event is the interview itself, and once it's complete, the opportunity is over. In actuality, you have great visibility opportunities you can harness by promoting the show beforehand and after . . . and you can even share it strategically months later when the subject fits a monthly theme or ties into a speaking engagement or summit you are doing. You can keep using and repurposing the interview strategically.

I have found that approximately 90 to 95 percent of listeners actually like to listen on demand . . . so not necessarily when the interview is being produced live or aired for the first time, but when it is convenient for them to listen to it. If you neglect to share the replay out, you could be missing 90 to 95 percent of your potential listening audience.

- Promote the show beforehand on social media and to your list. Make sure to tag the interviewer so that they see you are promoting and sharing. Their followers will see you, too. This builds a great connection with the host.

- Add the replay of your show to your website. Media loves media. So the more other potential interviewers, people who are thinking of hiring/working with you, and events looking for guests can see that you have been on multiple programs and shows . . . and can see/experience a sample of you being interviewed . . . the more they can truly see and appreciate you and your expertise. Plus, this builds trust with other media platforms and show hosts, as they can now see you are able to hold the space positively and well. They tend to like to have guests on their shows who are experienced and know how to play well.

- Share the replay out on social media and with your followers. If you are too busy to share the replay out, then you are too busy to do the interview in the first place. Sharing the replay is just as important as doing the interview itself. You want to actively promote and share the replay. Don't keep your fabulous interview that is showcasing you a secret. Share it out.

- Leveraging tips when sharing the replay:

- Always tag the host so they can see you sharing out the show and partnering with them in getting the message out.

- Add in a comment when you share out to create engagement . . . something like, "I loved the interview with XXX! My favorite part was . . . ." or "I shared a tip to help you XXXX." And then say, "I would love to know your thoughts about this." This gives people something to listen for and respond to.

- And . . . even if people don't listen to the full show . . . they know simply by your sharing that you are an expert in your field who is in demand and a go-to person to interview and share about your area of expertise. ☺

PRO TIP #7: HAVE A PLAN FOR THE INTERVIEW—BEFORE, DURING AND AFTER.

This means know the type of shows you want to be on, schedule them in such a way that you are able to prepare ahead of time, be fully present during the interview, and be able to share the replay once the show has been recorded and the replay is available. Know why you are on the show, who you hope to serve . . . and how you will strategically share out after the show.

- Be mindful of how many interviews you are scheduling a week/month/quarter . . . don't spread yourself too thin.

- Have a focus for each show. I recommend having a note card or note page for each show that you can quickly refer to . . . showing what the show is about, your focus for the show (make sure it ties into what you are wanting to focus on that month), and whether you're offering a free gift (if so, note what it is). This way, at a glance you can have all the key details of the show . . . including what you are focusing on talking about during your interview. Prepare this information when you schedule the interview so you aren't left scrambling right before. You will come across professionally and in an expert or pro way when you show up clear, focused and prepared for the interview.

- Write out the three key bullet points you want to make sure to cover/discuss during the show . . . then review the notes a couple days prior to the show and the morning of. Then you will be fully and powerfully prepared.

- At the end of the show, take a few minutes to write down key thoughts from the interview that stood out for you. This way you will easily be able to refer back to that when you share the replay out . . . and if you want to share it down the road, you'll already know key points you can highlight to create powerful engagement.

- Keep up the relationship. I do a quick debrief call with my guest(s) shortly after the show to check in with them on their experience and get feedback. And I give them information about harnessing the benefits of sharing out the replays. From these calls, I have learned that guests often don't share the replays because they feel uncomfortable about something about their performance or something they said during the show. What's so interesting to me is that, often, what happened was actually one of the most brilliant moments in the show! It's where they stretched, got vulnerable, and connected powerfully and humanly. And it's the thing someone will remember. When I share this with them, they get excited about their brilliance, and it becomes a powerful moment for them, and it builds our relationship as I hold that space for them.

Bonus Pro Tip:

Take a few minutes prior to the show to stop, pause, and breathe deeply. Remind yourself that you are the expert in this space, and you have been called to share this information. Trust that what will serve at the highest level will come forward in the conversation. You were made for such a time as this. As you breathe, release any anxiety/nerves. Remember, it is more about how you show up and hold the space than the exact words you say. Trust the interview process, and let your brilliance, heart and spirit SHINE!

Rebecca Hall Gruyter

Rebecca Hall Gruyter is a global influencer, a #1 international bestselling author, a compiler and publisher (helping over 1,000 authors become best sellers), a radio show host (reaching over 1 million listeners on 8 networks), and an empowerment leader. She has built multiple platforms to help experts reach more people. These platforms include radio, podcasts, books, magazines, the Speaker Talent Search, and live events, creating a powerful promotional reach of over 10 million!

Rebecca is the CEO of RHG Media Productions, the founder of Your Purpose Driven Practice, and the creator of the Speaker Talent Search. Rebecca has personally contributed to 40+ published books and multiple magazines, and she has been quoted in major media including Huffington Post, ABC, CBS, NBC, Fox, and Thrive Global. Today, she wants you to be seen, be heard, and SHINE!

    Email: Rebecca@YourPurposeDrivenPractice.com
    Websites and Social Media:
    http://www.YourPurposeDrivenPractice.com
    http://www.RHGTVNetwork.com
    http://www.SpeakerTalentSearch.com
    https://www.facebook.com/rhallgruyter
    https://www.linkedin.com/in/rebecca-hall-gruyter-2802669/
    http://www.x.com/Rebeccahgruyter
    https://www.instagram.com/rhg_global_community/
    http://www.EmpoweringWomenTransformingLives.com
    http://www.rebeccahallgruyter.linktoexpert.com/

Section 3:
Grow Your Visibility

Chapter 7
Authors, Keep the Momentum Going
by Rebecca Hall Gruyter

You have launched your beautiful book and released it out into the world! Congratulations! Now, you need to keep the momentum going! It's a myth that you write it and they will come. You are the one who gets to maintain the excitement and direct traffic on an ongoing basis to your book. You hold the power. ☺ You get to keep the momentum going, drive sales and build your own success. In this chapter, I share some tips to help you keep the momentum going that you had as you first released your powerful book to the world.

I often get asked, "Is there a shelf life for my book?" How long can an author expect to get visibility and marketing value from their book once it's been launched? If they did a bestselling campaign, how long will that visibility and momentum last? These are great questions, and exploring the answers can affect your business growth in positive and exciting ways!

First of all, the nature of your book might determine its shelf life and momentum. If the content is highly time-sensitive, that could shorten its value or interest in the public's mind. It might be a topic in an industry that's changing rapidly so you could create a very high impact in the medium term, which just might be the outcome you are looking for. Or you could choose to make your book content "evergreen" (more general and less time-sensitive), which might bring broader appeal and reach.

These are things you want to think about as you're writing your book. You're the one driving the content and your public's experience with the important message you are bringing to the world. It's your choice as the messenger of your gifts!

Of course, you can't always predict what the market, or the world, will be like when you launch your book. So, you do your best to share your message and make decisions that will deliver its highest impact to those who need to hear it.

My advice on this? Write to your people and your purpose, expect the unpredictable, and be ready to face and leverage opportunities that come!

How do I keep the marketing going after my book launch?

What I find in many new authors is that they are so excited about the launch—there's a flurry of activity, and they're loving the visibility, actually seeing their book appear on Amazon and other platforms, following the sales, and witnessing the rise to bestseller or international bestseller status. It's all good!

There's another exciting phase when the print version comes out and it is promoted as well. The marketing we started back in the early stages of producing the book, then these two launches, generate much attention and business growth for the author.

However, some authors stop promoting their books at this point. They stop sharing or strategizing, and it all dies. They forget that it's important to build a strategy to continue to promote and share about their book on an ongoing basis.

They don't realize that their book can continue to promote their brand and grow their business. They can keep driving the conversation, increasing awareness and visibility. The truth is that over time, the book will not stand on its own no matter how amazing it is.

Here are some ways to keep the momentum going long after the book experiences its first launch and to gain even more traction for your business growth. You must also continue to market and share out. That is how you build the buzz and momentum around your book and continue the momentum.

1. **During the book launch, take screenshots of significant things** that happened during the launch—ranking numbers growing, readers' reviews and accolades sent to the author, media recognition, for example. This is what I do with my clients. Then we repurpose the screenshots by sharing them out. People love to see them and be part of the author's journey. We use the momentum from the very beginning of the author's process to build engagement with the content and anticipation of what's coming next.

2. **Ask for and share out reviews in social media.** Thank people who write reviews, even if you don't know them. Also let people know that you would love to know their thoughts on your book, and include the link to where they can purchase and leave a review, too. These are great ways to lift others up and show appreciation as well as to increase your visibility and get more reviews for your book.

3. **Have opportunities for people to get added to your list so you can connect with them on an ongoing basis . . . use the book launch as a way to grow your list.** Perhaps encourage people to take a picture of themselves with your book and share it out in social media along with their review.

4. **Repurpose content from the book and share it out in different formats** to direct people back to the book or to your services and offerings. Here are some of my favorite ideas—the sky's the creative limit!

    - Take chapters from your book and adapt them to blog articles shared on your website, LinkedIn, or other writing platforms.

    - Include cited book content in social media and newsletters to your list.

    - Create a video series or online tele-class using the content of the book, and of course include an invitation to purchase.

- Adapt your book content to become an online course in itself, potentially being offered for years.

- Use a written chapter as a bonus or giveaway in a package or program you are offering. For example, a chapter is something you can offer as a free gift when you are making a guest appearance on a podcast, TV, or radio show.

- Reserve copies of your print-version book to give away for free in the same places I listed above. Especially when your book sales (finally) taper off, your book will still serve as a marketing tool. By the way, at this point it might be time to write a new one.

- All these options drive engagement and future sales. As long as the content and story you have written are relevant to the people you want to reach, you can continue to repurpose them in all of these and other creative ways!

5. **Make an audio version of your book to bring a whole other experience to the reader.** Besides offering an opportunity for an audio book launch, you then can offer free downloads of clips or chapters from the book to continue marketing in the ways I describe above. Every time you release a new format of your book or a new book, you can use that as an opportunity to bring your book and its content to the forefront of people's minds again, and you will want to drive traffic to your book and all its formats. This helps more and more people know about your book and gives them the opportunity to share it out and get their copy in their favorite format.

6. **Have an ongoing promotion plan.**

    a. **In social media.** Have a focus each month, tied into monthly themes, and break it into weekly shares about your book . . . maybe sharing a review, a screenshot from the campaign, a success story, a favorite part of the book, or a tip that people can discover more about in your book. Keep bringing your book and content forward on a weekly basis . . . keep it top of mind for people.

    b. **When speaking or being interviewed.** Remember, there are always new people in the audience. Make sure to mention your book and where to get it. Don't assume people already know. Leverage that you are a published author, and be proud to share about your book.

c. **When networking.** It could be as simple as introducing yourself. "Hi, I'm XXXXXXX, author of XXXXXX." This instantly positions you, helps brand the book with you, and will frequently lead to follow-up questions where people will want to know more about your book.

d. **Have a book signing party.** You can create an event around your book and invite people to it . . . signing, celebrating and sharing. People love meeting authors and learning more about them and why they brought their book forward. This could even be a space where you share additional ways they can work with you or get on your list, and it can potentially lead into programs or services that you offer in addition to your book.

e. **Develop a program around your book.** Develop a program that people will want to sign up for or get assistance with as they read your book. *(And make sure to mention it in your book...and include a way people can contact you to sign up or learn more.)* People who read your book will frequently be inspired and would love to have the opportunity to go deeper with you. Let them know how to do so . . . don't assume they will automatically know.

f. **Lead a book reading program.** Create a virtual program/group/community in which you lead people through your book chapter by chapter. Make reading a social activity.

g. **Do a video series to tie into your book or bring additional content forward.** Your published book has established you as an expert in your space. You can build on that by bringing in additional content, series, or programs forward. You can even share videos periodically in which you give updates in your area of expertise and remind people about getting their copy today to discover, learn, etc.

Be creative and have fun. You can create so much and build so many things from your powerful book. Remember to keep sharing and keep bringing it forward. The power and choice are in your hands.

Personal RHG note: *Here is a story of an author whose book momentum shifted dramatically and how we pivoted in a positive way. One of my clients wrote an important book in the healthcare space which was released in 2018. They were doing a great amount of speaking and book signings, gaining wonderful traction on the book. Then, in 2020, the coronavirus pandemic happened, and the whole healthcare industry was turned on its head. The author of course did not want to create a whole new book, but we also wanted to address the new need for information and get it out in a timely way.*

So, they created a video series with this information, bringing in industry experts. They still promoted the book from our original plan, but adding this series created another market space helping people navigate the new waters in a timely and helpful way. This series still directed people to the book and provided another way to drive traffic, grow their reach, and grow their list—while supporting people in challenging times. It was a great success and helped the author keep the momentum going and continue to serve their people while driving traffic/sales to their empowering and important book.

Pro tip: Have a 6-month and 12-month strategy to plot out these different ways of making your book work for your business. Try things out and then assess, update, and tweak them based on the feedback you receive. The most important thing is to keep in touch with what your community wants—your current and potential clients, sponsors, supporters, etc.

You spend so much time, energy and expertise in creating, writing and publishing your book. Make sure to keep sharing about it so that you can reach as many people as possible with your transformational information and messages. You are in control and can choose to keep the momentum going. Be willing to have your book be easy to find as you share it out proudly and purposefully into the world. May you and your book SHINE!

Remember, what the world needs is more of you!

Rebecca Hall Gruyter

Rebecca Hall Gruyter is a global influencer, a #1 international bestselling author, a compiler and publisher (helping over 1,000 authors become bestsellers), a radio show host (reaching over 1 million listeners on 8 networks), and an empowerment leader. She has built multiple platforms to help experts reach more people. These platforms include radio, podcasts, books, magazines, the Speaker Talent Search, and live events, creating a powerful promotional reach of over 10 million!

Rebecca is the CEO of RHG Media Productions, the founder of Your Purpose Driven Practice, and the creator of the Speaker Talent Search. Rebecca has personally contributed to 40+ published books and multiple magazines, and she has been quoted in major media including Huffington Post, ABC, CBS, NBC, Fox, and Thrive Global. Today, she wants you to be seen, be heard, and SHINE!

Email: Rebecca@YourPurposeDrivenPractice.com
Websites and Social Media:
http://www.YourPurposeDrivenPractice.com
http://www.RHGTVNetwork.com
http://www.SpeakerTalentSearch.com
https://www.facebook.com/rhallgruyter
https://www.linkedin.com/in/rebecca-hall-gruyter-2802669/
http://www.x.com/Rebeccahgruyter
https://www.instagram.com/rhg_global_community/
http://www.EmpoweringWomenTransformingLives.com
http://www.rebeccahallgruyter.linktoexpert.com/

CHAPTER 8
FAST-TRACK YOUR SUCCESS WITH ANTHOLOGIES
BY REBECCA HALL GRUYTER

What makes a book an anthology? An anthology is a collection of works by multiple authors, each writing a section or chapter on a common theme. *You can fast-track your visibility and bring forward your message by participating in anthologies.* The compiler leads the book project, supports the co-authors in helping them write their chapters, and provides editing, formatting, publishing, and promotion for the book. When you contribute to an anthology, you are working in a supportive community, being guided step-by-step through the process of becoming a published author with a built-in marketing strategy to share your message out with the world—**all for a fraction of the time, cost and energy of a full book production.**

<u>**There are several benefits of contributing to an anthology as a writer:**</u>

1. If you've never written a book before, the idea of producing 200 or more pages can feel daunting. Writing a chapter or two for an anthology is less overwhelming and a great way to break into book writing.

Plus, it helps you start to bring your content forward and out into the world . . . or helps you bring additional or new content forward. The writing commitment for a chapter in an anthology is typically 1,500 to 2,500 words, rather than 60,000+ words to write an entire book on your own—a bit more manageable!

2. You become a published author, giving you credibility and visibility. This status often gives you a foot in the door to publishers, magazines, and other forms of media to whom you would like to submit more of your writing.

3. It's a wonderful sense of accomplishment and pride to see your name and your ideas in a book that will reach readers who need to hear your powerful message.

4. A book with your name in it is a powerful marketing tool to expand your influence and grow your business, both during the launch and on an ongoing basis. **Tip:** Look for an anthology that commits to doing a Bestselling Campaign . . . or, even better, one that guarantees the book will become a bestseller!

5. Anthologies have a high chance of becoming bestsellers because the compiler and all the contributors are doing their own marketing and selling the book to their own contacts. Strength in numbers! You get exposure to your co-authors' respective reaches and communities with your content and message . . . while they get exposure to yours. It's a win-win for all: a win for your message, for your reach, and for those who will now know about you.

6. The experience of writing for publication exercises your writing muscles and strengthens your ability to pull together your ideas, gifts, messages, and expertise in a structured, powerful form. You get to learn about the book publishing and launching process as you participate—one chapter at a time.

7. You are able to become a published author for about one-tenth to one-fifth of the cost and time it would take you to produce and publish a full book on your own.

8. Once the book has been released, you can repurpose your chapter and use it as a free gift to grow your list. Your powerful information has now been edited, formatted and professionally published, and you can use your chapter as a giveaway, sell it, or do anything else you want to do with it. ☺ **Tip:** Make sure the anthology you choose to participate in still has you retain all rights to your content . . . and know what timeframe they have for you to wait (if any) before repurposing your chapter.

How the Anthology Process Works

Depending on the compiler, you typically pay to be part of the anthology. In some cases, authors are required additionally to purchase a certain number of books themselves. Some compilers will publish an electronic version of the book as well as a print version. Some, but not all, specialize in the marketing and bestselling launch process.

As you look at opportunities to contribute to an anthology, it's very important to find out the nature of the arrangement. Ask questions about the options I listed above to make sure you are clear about the compiler's expectations before you make a decision.

Also ask who owns the content you've written for the book, and how you are allowed to repurpose it or reproduce the chapter for your own marketing purposes. You want to be able to use your content later to share out your important message and grow your business.

The compiler will give you a list of writing guidelines to follow, such as:

- The theme or main topic of the book and who it is designed to reach and serve

- Maximum word count for your chapter and how many chapters you may submit

- Whether you are allowed to include links to your website, offerings, or other content within your chapter

- How your bio should be written

- Specs for your author photo

- What your responsibilities (and opportunities) will be to help market this book

- Style expectations for your chapter (for example, they may want you to add tips at the end of the chapter, focus on a particular subject, have a particular font style and size they want you to use, and possibly a layout/flow of how they want the chapter to include your bio and contact information.)

- Timelines and deadlines for submitting drafts and final versions

Make sure you are in alignment with the theme/topic of the book and understand the publisher's guidelines before you commit to the project.

Many compilers—or at least the ones you'll want to work with!—will support you through the process of writing your chapter, understanding the book publishing process, and involve you in the marketing and the exciting launch itself.

Is an Anthology Right For You?

Here are some things to consider before you jump in:

1. **You won't likely see your name on the front cover of the book.** You will be one of anywhere between ten and thirty other contributors. If you've never published before and you want your name on the cover of your own book, the anthology opportunity is a great step in that direction. Many writers love being in a community with like-minded people sharing their brilliant interpretations of the topic, empowering all as a group. Frequently the compiler will list your name on the back cover (which is great for positioning and visibility).

2. **You will likely be investing some of your own money.** The truth is, book royalties are not going to make you lots of money, whether the book is an anthology or one written entirely by you. The real value of participating in an anthology is what you do with the book and how you leverage the visibility to grow your reach, grow your list, and drive traffic to your programs and offerings. (You can learn more in my free e-book *Top 3 Myths and Truths*

About Monetizing Your Book, available at https://yourpurposedrivenpractice.com/books/free-ebooks-emerging-authors.) Consider how the anthology option could be an investment in your longer-term business growth and see if there's a fit. It's an opportunity to become a published author while being positioned as an expert as you grow your reach and impact.

3. **Think strategically.** How can you write a chapter that aligns with your business, mission, and visibility goals as well as the compiler's vision for the anthology? Have you written any blog posts or articles that could possibly become part of your powerful chapter? Lastly, write your chapter in a way that makes it easy to repurpose later.

How an Anthology Can Work for You

The chapter you contribute to an anthology can become one of your favorite marketing tools:

- Your chapter will bring your name, expertise and content to the world.

- It's a "business card" you can use to seek opportunities to speak, be interviewed, and share your voice and brand.

- You can use it as a free gift to help people get to know you and sign up to be on your email list.

- You can showcase the anthology on your website for your visitors to see and buy, and you can link to it from your social media accounts.

- Once the book is released, you can repurpose your chapter as a downloadable PDF to put on your website as a free resource to stimulate inbound traffic, or you can bundle it with other valuable content for purchase and to grow your list.

- You can reference the anthology during a talk or interview, along with a link for your audience to download it (thus capturing their names and email addresses for your list).

- Your chapter can keep on bringing value as you find new creative ways to use it.

Anthologies Aren't Just for New, Unpublished Writers

Many authors who have published on their own still like to participate in anthologies. It helps create additional content that they can use to lead new groups of people to their programs or their other books. It's a great marketing strategy and approach.

Each chapter you contribute to an anthology can be repurposed and used as a gift to grow your list, as a giveaway, or a bonus with your programs . . . or a great way to reach out to potential clients, introducing them to you and your content while giving them some great tips . . . positioning you as the go-to expert they want to work with and/or learn more from. I've seen full programs built around anthology projects that take the co-authors on a transformational journey and empower them to share their gifts and talents with the world.

It can be powerful to step into the compiler role and lead an anthology project, too. "One of our authors is on her third anthology with us," Cathy Davis of Creative Publishing Partners says. "She told me how doing anthologies has helped to grow her business, building relationships with her readers and her co-authors."

Personal RHG note: Even though I'm a number one international bestselling author many times over, I still participate in anthologies, both as a contributing writer and as a compiler. I love to see how a community of authors happens with each anthology group. The co-authors cheer each other on. They build rapport and relationships, and they stay connected even after the book has been released and launched. Plus, it helps me build new relationships, expand my reach, and continue to grow my library of chapters with current content to share with the world. In this way I create more offerings for my list-growing library of free gifts. It also lets me work with writers who are committed to bringing their message forward to make a positive difference in the world—it's very rewarding for me personally and professionally!

Pro tip: Be an active participant and receptive learner in the anthology-writing experience. Look to—and trust—the compiler and their experts who are invested in making this book successful. You will learn a lot about writing and about the publishing world that will serve you in the future. Also, remember the "strength in numbers" I mentioned. You and your co-authors are responsible for marketing the book to your own networks so that, together, everyone can succeed.

Choose to stand up and be seen in the anthology community, and fully participate in the launch . . . it's a great opportunity to be seen as a leader of leaders. Remember to repurpose your powerful chapter to grow your list and impact as many people as possible on an ongoing basis. Your voice, your chapter, and your message matter and are needed in the world!

Remember, what the world needs is more of you! My passion is to help new and seasoned authors expand their reach and influence to impact more people, one heart at a time.

Rebecca Hall Gruyter

Rebecca Hall Gruyter is a global influencer, a #1 international bestselling author, a compiler and publisher (helping over 1,000 authors become bestsellers), a radio show host (reaching over 1 million listeners on 8 networks), and an empowerment leader. She has built multiple platforms to help experts reach more people. These platforms include radio, podcasts, books, magazines, the Speaker Talent Search, and live events, creating a powerful promotional reach of over 10 million!

Rebecca is the CEO of RHG Media Productions, the founder of Your Purpose Driven Practice, and the creator of the Speaker Talent Search. Rebecca has personally contributed to 40+ published books and multiple magazines, and she has been quoted in major media including Huffington Post, ABC, CBS, NBC, Fox, and Thrive Global. Today, she wants you to be seen, be heard, and SHINE!

Email: Rebecca@YourPurposeDrivenPractice.com
Websites and Social Media:
http://www.YourPurposeDrivenPractice.com
http://www.RHGTVNetwork.com
http://www.SpeakerTalentSearch.com
https://www.facebook.com/rhallgruyter
https://www.linkedin.com/in/rebecca-hall-gruyter-2802669/
http://www.x.com/Rebeccahgruyter
https://www.instagram.com/rhg_global_community/
http://www.EmpoweringWomenTransformingLives.com
http://www.rebeccahallgruyter.linktoexpert.com/

Chapter 9
Show Hosting Tips for Success
by Rebecca Hall Gruyter

Congratulations on being the host of your own show. Whether you are a new show or podcast host or you have had your weekly show for over ten years with hundreds of episodes under your belt . . . I celebrate you. Thank you for leaning in and creating a powerful platform to reach more people and make an ongoing impact with your words, energy, insights, guests and content.

I believe one of the most powerful ways you can show up in the world is as a speaker. When you lead your own show, you get to have as many speaking opportunities as you want as often as you want . . . giving you endless opportunities to impact others with your messages. You can serve your listeners/viewers/community each and every week of your show, one episode at a time. This gives you the opportunity to build your followers and influence episode by episode, heart by heart, with intention and purpose. How you show up makes a difference. I encourage you to be strategic and intentional with what you bring forward.

I have found it such an honor and privilege leading my own show, *Empowering Women, Transforming Lives*, for over ten years now. It is broadcast live and syndicated as a podcast on multiple platforms and networks. I've had the honor of leading multiple shows a week in the form of live events, virtual summits, and a variety of different weekly shows at time as well as being a guest on multiple platforms and stages. With well over 1,500 episodes under my belt, I have found that being a host has helped me grow personally and professionally. I build meaningful connections, and I learn from my guests every single week. Hosting has helped me build a wonderful community and following to grow my business, expand my reach and influence, network powerfully, and open doors to amazing opportunities.

Today, I wanted to share some of my top success tips . . . including a couple of leveraging tips I have discovered and have trained many hosts on using to build the success of their shows. I hope they help you grow your following, reach, business, list, connections, and client base, leading you to new and exciting opportunities.

Show Hosting Success Tips

1. **Have a schedule and stick to it.**

Nothing alienates an audience faster than being inconsistent about when new episodes appear. A big part of showing consideration for your listeners/viewers and building trust with them is putting out your content on a consistent schedule. People want to know when new episodes are available to enjoy. If they have to keep checking and hoping, they will soon lose interest and find another show to follow that is consistent about providing the content that they enjoy . . . and can count on being released consistently.

2. **Be present.**

Being a host takes practice, and you only get it one way: by actually doing it in that live space. In the beginning you may feel uncertain, not really in control, and perhaps lost in the midst of all that's going on. That's okay. You'll learn something each time simply by doing it, literally building all these new neural pathways that will take you to excellence. As a new host, you're learning to lead, manage the time, get directions from the tech team and/or do some tech yourself, have the next questions ready, and control the direction of the show.

BUT, you also need to be present throughout to bring your viewers/listeners the best possible experience. Being present means listening to your guests and allowing yourself the opportunity to be truly in the moment. Be open to conversation opportunities or inspiration as you lead your show. Allow yourself room to follow a new direction in conversation when you feel it will serve your listeners.

3. **Experiment.**

Don't be afraid to experiment to find your lane and your unique brand. Try different ways to open or close the show until you find what works best for you and your viewers/listeners.

4. **Be ready for the unexpected.**

Lots of things can go wrong with a live or prerecorded show: tech problems, a late guest, a conversation beginning to get out of hand, the engineer making a mistake and delaying cutting to the break. Open yourself to go with the flow of the experience, and you won't get thrown off.

5. **Have an outline for each episode.**

Make a one-page outline for each episode that lists bullet points and how much time you have allotted for each. Keep this outline (and a clock) in view during the show. You are the director, the orchestrator of your show, so you get to create the experience for yourself, your listeners, and your guests. You're invested in the show because of your brand, your reputation, and the service you want to bring to the world. Having an outline ensures you will get to everything you need to in order to make the show a great experience for all.

You can still allow room for the organic conversation and flow . . . but having an outline/plan to follow enables you to consistently deliver value to your listeners/viewers while giving your guest room to shine (if you have guests). When you make an outline, you are better able to share about the subject matter and discuss it in a balanced way. You don't want to run out of time for a key point because you talked too long about a point earlier in the show. An outline helps you bring everything forward you are looking to share and bring forward in your show.

Your show should reflect YOU, to let you shine as you let your guests shine. You make the choice of the theme and how you want to open and close the show. You decide if you would like one or multiple guests, how you want to structure your interview, and a specific way you engage them at the end. Be creative and make it yours!

Once you have the structure of your program, it's important to make sure you stay on track during your show. Here are tips to help:

- Try to keep your outline on one sheet so that you're not crinkling papers, which will be distracting to the audience.

- Keep your bullet points short enough so you can just glance down and stay present, especially if it's a video show.

- Have a pen handy to take notes during the show so you can summarize the highlights at the end or come back to something a guest just said that rocked your world (you get to grow, too!).

Be intentional and strategic, but do not overly rehearse or you'll take all the life out of your show. Remember, it's not a presentation—it's a live, organic exchange between you, your guest, and every listener out there. Your goal is to stay present, focused, and listening so you can glance down at your list, see what's next, and choose to go in that direction or a different one with your guest. I might jot down one word to jog my memory, but generally I choose to stay present. The listening and retaining come with practice.

6. **Consider scheduling multiple guests per show (leveraging tip!!!).**

I have found that having two guests per show is a powerful way to grow my reach exponentially. Not only does it give me an opportunity to have twice as many people sharing out about the show to their reach and list, it also ensures I will have a guest to interview if for some reason one of my guests isn't able to show up. When this happens, the show still goes on, and the remaining guest is usually excited because they get more airtime and room on the show to share. This helps me stick to my schedule for releasing new shows, which means I grow my reach and list faster . . . plus, each guest gets to share their message with my audience, their audience, and that of the other guest as well. Reaching more people is a win for all.

7. **It's your show. Own it.**

As they say about most performances, start strong and end strong! Approach every show with confidence, take care of your energy (you'll need it!), and commit to ending with that same confidence. That's what people will remember. Keep the reins on the conversation and your vision and boundaries strong.

I once received expert advice from my mentor, Robert Ciolino, that changed everything for me: "Rebecca, when a guest is talking too long and interrupting you and starting to go off in a way that no longer serves your listeners, always choose your listeners, not the guest. Shut the guest down, lovingly and firmly."

He said this because guests who were running wild and taking over the show were alienating my audience. Your audience are the ones who come back week after week to attend your show. They are the ones you are serving. They are the people you're taking a stand for and representing. So, if you ever have to choose, always choose your listeners. Stand for them and have clear boundaries with your guests. They are guests, but it is your show and your listeners/viewers.

8. **Set your guests, your show, and yourself up for success.**

You shine when your guests shine! Set the tone and prepare the "stage" for your guest to feel comfortable, confident, and prepared.

The best way I've found to help my guests shine is to prepare their expectations—and mine—ahead of time. This is what I do; create your own approach for the type of show you are hosting:

- I invite guests to send in their questions ahead of time. This can include questions they would like to be asked as well as any questions they have about the process of guesting on my show.

- I ask my guests to listen to two or three episodes of my show to get a feel for the flow.

- I get their contact information.

- I invite the guest (or guests) to join two or three minutes before we go live. I welcome them by saying, "I'm excited you're here!"

- I let them know how the show is going to work. For example, I might say: "In the opening segment, I will be doing most of the talking as I lead a short meditation. Then I will welcome you and give you ten or fifteen seconds to do a quick share in response to the meditation. Then we will go to our first commercial break."

- During the break, I give them additional instruction, such as: "I will introduce you as XXXX and summarize your background. After that, I'll ask you some of the questions you suggested. Then I will ask you a few questions of my own."

- I ask them to please keep their answers to 90 seconds or less, so we can get through all of their beautiful content; otherwise they may only get through their first answer before we have to go to break.

- I tell them that if they're going a little long, which is easy to do when we're passionate, I will give them a cue by softly interrupting. I explain that if I do this, it means bring the sentence to a close, not the paragraph.

- During the ad breaks, I check in with them so they know what to expect in each segment (and we often laugh a lot as we chat).

- I let them know that we leave the contact links and info until the end, and they'll have 60 seconds or less to share that information before we close so that the show can end on time.

My guests love knowing what to expect, and I haven't had any "guests gone wild" in a long time. My audience is happy and so am I!

9. Promote your show.

It's in everybody's best interest to promote and share before, during, and after the show. I have found that 95 to 97% of people are listening to replays, playing on demand. So after the initial airing of the show, we continue to promote the replay, and we encourage our guests to do the same.

The beauty of online program platforms is that their reach is endless, and you want to leverage that opportunity as much as you can. Be direct with your guests about asking them to share out the show and the replay, and make it easy for them to do so. Most guests don't share because they don't realize that it matters or they are uncomfortable about something that they shared/said on the show. Encourage your guests to harness the benefits of the show replays and incorporate them into their marketing. Let them know what they shared that was brilliant and encourage them to share out.

10. Do a debrief (another leveraging tip!).

After a guest appears on your show, check in with them to keep up the relationship. I do a quick debrief call with my guest(s) shortly after the show to ask how their experience was and to get their feedback. (This is when I reiterate the information about harnessing the benefits of sharing out the replays.)

In these calls, I have discovered that guests often don't share the replays because they feel uncomfortable about something about their performance or something they said during the show. What I have found interesting over the years is that the thing they are most uncomfortable about on the show tends to be one of the most brilliant moments in the show! It's where they stretched, got vulnerable, and connected powerfully and humanly. And it's the thing someone will remember. When I share this with them, they get excited about their brilliance and it becomes a powerful moment for them, and it builds our relationship as I hold that space for them.

At the end of the debrief call, I ask if there is anything else the guest has questions about or wants to connect about. This question has led to a lot of new clients, referrals, business opportunities, interviews, and speaking opportunities. We have just had this powerful experience together on my show, where they have gotten to shine beautifully with space being held for them and their message. The guests are excited about additional ways we can connect and work together.

I hope these tips help you build your list, your following, your connections, and your business. Enjoy bringing your show forward and know that each episode makes a powerful difference. The world will be brighter, more empowered, and a more uplifted place because you leaned in to serve others with your show. May you expand your reach, share your message and shine brightly out into the world!

Rebecca Hall Gruyter

Rebecca Hall Gruyter is a global influencer, a #1 international bestselling author, a compiler and publisher (helping over 1,000 authors become bestsellers), a radio show host (reaching over 1 million listeners on 8 networks), and an empowerment leader. She has built multiple platforms to help experts reach more people. These platforms include radio, podcasts, books, magazines, the Speaker Talent Search, and live events, creating a powerful promotional reach of over 10 million!

Rebecca is the CEO of RHG Media Productions, the founder of Your Purpose Driven Practice, and the creator of the Speaker Talent Search. Rebecca has personally contributed to 40+ published books and multiple magazines, and she has been quoted in major media including Huffington Post, ABC, CBS, NBC, Fox, and Thrive Global. Today, she wants you to be seen, be heard, and SHINE!

Email: Rebecca@YourPurposeDrivenPractice.com
Websites and Social Media:
http://www.YourPurposeDrivenPractice.com
http://www.RHGTVNetwork.com
http://www.SpeakerTalentSearch.com
https://www.facebook.com/rhallgruyter
https://www.linkedin.com/in/rebecca-hall-gruyter-2802669/
http://www.x.com/Rebeccahgruyter
https://www.instagram.com/rhg_global_community/
http://www.EmpoweringWomenTransformingLives.com
http://www.rebeccahallgruyter.linktoexpert.com/

Quotes to Encourage and Inspire You

Quotes That Inspire Mary Struzinsky

"Vulnerability is a risk, but it's the only path to deeper connections and meaningful experiences."
  —Brené Brown

"Fear and caution are two different things. Be cautious—be conscious—but do not be fearful. Fear only paralyzes, while consciousness mobilizes. Be mobilized, not paralyzed."
  —Donald Walsch

"Procrastination is not a problem with managing time; it is a problem with managing emotions. Manage your emotions, not your time."
  —Joel Brown

"Doubt kills more dreams than failure ever will."
  —<u>Suzy Kassem</u>

"Always ask yourself the question, is this going to help me get to my goal or not?"
  —Bob Proctor

Inspirational Quote by Mary Struzinsky

"Your struggles do not reflect a flaw in your character, but a testament to your humanity. You are not broken; you are beautifully human. When you let go of what drains you, and embrace what illuminates you, you will discover the power to shine brilliantly in every facet of your life."
  —Mary Struzinsky

Quotes That Inspire Deborah Wiener

"The privilege of a lifetime is to become who you truly are."
—C.G. Jung

"What you are living is the evidence of what you are thinking and feeling, every single time."
—Abraham Hicks

"Change your thoughts and you change your world."
—Norman Vincent Peale

"Compassionate people ask for what they need. They say no when they need to, and when they say yes, they mean it. They're compassionate because their boundaries keep them out of resentment."
—Brené Brown

"Your visibility encourages others to step into their own power and authenticity."
—Marianne Williamson

Inspirational Quotes by Deborah Wiener

"By discovering your genuine, authentic self, a world of possibilities and potential suddenly opens."
—Deborah Wiener

"Where Energy Flows, Money Goes!"
—Deborah Wiener

Quotes That Inspire Maureen Ryan Blake

"Why fit in when you were born to stand out?"
—Dr. Seuss

"Imagination is more important than knowledge. For knowledge is limited, whereas imagination embraces the entire world, stimulating progress, giving birth to evolution."
—Albert Einstein

"When you reach the end of your rope, tie a knot in it and hang on."
—Franklin D. Roosevelt

"The future belongs to those who believe in the beauty of their dreams."
—Eleanor Roosevelt

"You will face many defeats in life, but never let yourself be defeated."
—Maya Angelou

Inspirational Quote by Maureen Ryan Blake
"When a woman loses her tribe, she loses her shine. But when we come together, we shine brighter."
—Maureen Ryan Blake

QUOTES THAT INSPIRE REBECCA HALL GRUYTER

"Be yourself; everyone else is already taken."
—Oscar Wilde

"Two roads diverged in a wood, and I—I took the one less traveled by, and that has made all the difference."
—Robert Frost

"The only place success comes before work is in the dictionary."
—Vince Lombardi

"Life is 10% what happens to me and 90% how I react to it."
—Charles Swindoll

"You miss 100% of the shots you don't take."
—Wayne Gretzky

"When everything seems to be going against you, remember that the airplane takes off against the wind, not with it."
—Henry Ford

"Most people fail in life not because they aim too high and miss, but because they aim too low and hit."
—Lee Brown

"You become what you believe."
—Oprah Winfrey

"I'm a success today because I had a friend who believed in me and I didn't have the heart to let them down."
—Abraham Lincoln

"Promise me you will always remember: you're braver than you believe, and stronger than you seem, and smarter than you think."
—Christopher Robin to Winnie the Pooh, as written by A.A. Milne

"In the middle of difficulty lies opportunity."
　—Albert Einstein

"All our dreams can come true, if we have the courage to pursue them."
　—Walt Disney

"You were designed for accomplishment, engineered for success, and endowed with the seeds of greatness!"
　—Zig Ziglar

"The question isn't who is going to let me; it's who is going to stop me."
　—Ayn Rand

"Start where you are. Use what you have. Do what you can."
　—Arthur Ashe

"Act as if what you do makes a difference. It does."
　—William James

"Problems are not stop signs, they are guidelines."
　—Robert Schuller

"God's work done in God's way will never lack God's supplies."
　—Hudson Taylor

QUOTES BY REBECCA HALL GRUYTER

"Life is not a solo journey."
—Rebecca Hall Gruyter

"Be willing to bloom where you are planted and SHINE!"
—Rebecca Hall Gruyter

"Choose to live on purpose and with purpose."
—Rebecca Hall Gruyter

"The greatest gift you can give the world is more of you. Choose to share the gift of you; SHINE!"
—Rebecca Hall Gruyter

"You must be willing to be seen on the same level you want to serve."
—Rebecca Hall Gruyter

Closing Thoughts

We hope you have been touched by these powerful chapters that have encouraged, equipped and empowered you to embrace *Visibility Today*! We can't wait to see you, hear from you, and celebrate you as you share your gift of you with the world! May you always choose to **live on purpose and with great purpose.**

Anthologies Compiled by Rebecca Hall Gruyter:

SHINE Series (compiled and led by Rebecca Hall Gruyter)
  Come Out of Hiding and SHINE! (Book 1)
  Bloom Where You Are Planted and SHINE! (Book 2)
  Step Forward and SHINE! (Book 3)

Brilliance Series (compiled and led by Rebecca Hall Gruyter)
  Step Into Your Brilliance! (Book 1)
  Step Into Your Brilliant Purpose! (Book 2)
  Share Your Brilliance! (Book 3)

Experts and Influencers Series (compiled and led by Rebecca Hall Gruyter)
  Experts and Influencers Series: Leadership (Book 1)
  Experts and Influencers Series: Women's Empowerment (Book 2)
  Experts and Influencers Series: Step Forward With Purpose (Book 3)

Visibility Today! (anthology compiled by Rebecca Hall Gruyter)

The Grandmother Legacies (anthology compiled by Rebecca Hall Gruyter)

The Animal Legacies (anthology compiled by Rebecca Hall Gruyter)

Bloom & SHINE! (365 daily inspiration anthology compiled by Rebecca Hall Gruyter)

Empowering YOU, Transforming Lives (365 daily inspiration anthology compiled by Rebecca Hall Gruyter)

JOURNALS BY REBECCA HALL GRUYTER:

The Animal Legacies Journal

The Experts and Influencers Leadership Journal

The Experts and Influencers Women's Empowerment Journal

The Experts and Influencers Move Forward With Purpose Journal

Women's Empowerment Journal

Step Into Your Brilliance Journal

Step Into Your Brilliant Purpose Journal

Share Your Brilliance Journal

BOOKS FEATURING A CHAPTER BY REBECCA HALL GRUYTER:

The 40/40 Rules, anthology compiled by Holly Porter

Becoming Outrageously Successful, anthology compiled by Dr. Anita Jackson

Bright Spots, anthology compiled by Davis Creative

Catch Your Star, anthology published by THRIVE Publishing

Discover Your Destiny, anthology compiled by Denise Joy Thompson

Engaging Experts, anthology compiled by Davis Creative

I Am Beautiful, anthology compiled by Teresa Hawley-Howard

Movers & Shakers 2020, anthology compiled by Teresa Hawley-Howard

The Power of Our Voices, Sharing Our Story, anthology compiled by Teresa Hawley-Howard

Real Estate Investing for Women, anthology compiled by Moneeka Sawyer

Succeeding Against All Odds, anthology compiled by Sandra Yancey

Success Secrets for Today's Feminine Entrepreneurs, anthology compiled by Dr. Anita Jackson

The Unstoppable Woman of Purpose, anthology and workbook, compiled by Nella Chikwe

Women on a Mission, anthology compiled by Teresa Hawley-Howard

Women of Courage, Women of Destiny, anthology compiled by Dr. Anita Jackson

Women Warriors Who Make It Rock, anthology compiled by Nichole Peters

You Are Whole, Perfect, and Complete—Just as You Are, compiled by Carol Plummer and Susan Driscoll

Dear Powerful Reader,

Thank you for reading our anthology. We hope it has encouraged and empowered you and uplifted you in the area of leadership. Listed below, please find out a little bit more about the compiler that led the team to create this powerful book for you.

RHG Media Productions and Your Purpose Driven Practice™

I wanted to share a little bit more about our organizations, Your Purpose Driven Practice™, RHG TV Network™, RHG Publishing™, and RHG Media Productions™. We are passionate about helping others live on purpose and with purpose in their lives and businesses. I hope this book has supported and inspired you to choose to live on purpose and with great purpose in your leadership!

If you want to reach more people and be part of inspiring and supporting others with your message, your gifts, and the work that you bring to the world, then I want to share some opportunities for you to consider.

Each year we compile and produce anthology book projects, support authors in publishing their own powerful books as bestsellers, produce and publish an international magazine, facilitate women's empowerment conferences, get quoted in major media, launch radio and podcast shows, and help experts and speakers step into a place of powerful influence to make a global difference. We provide programs and strategies to help you reach more people, and we facilitate the Speaker Talent Search (which helps speakers, experts, and influencers connect with more speaking opportunities). We would love to support you in reaching more people. Please take a moment to learn a little bit more about us at the sites listed below, and then reach out to us for a conversation. **We would love to help you be seen, be heard, and SHINE!**

You can learn more about each of these things on our main website: www.YourPurposeDrivenPractice.com

Enjoy our powerful **TV and podcast shows**: www.RHGTVNetwork.com

Learn more about the **Speaker Talent Search**™: www.SpeakerTalentSearch.com

Learn more about our **writing opportunities**: http://yourpurposedriven-practice.com/writing-opportunities/

If you would like to connect with me personally to explore some of our opportunities in upcoming book projects, podcast/radio shows, and/or TV, then here is the link to schedule a time to speak with me directly: www.MeetWithRebecca.com, or you can email me at: Rebecca@YourPuposeDrivenPractice.com.

May you always choose to be seen, be heard, and SHINE!

Warmly,

Rebecca Hall Gruyter
Compiler and Empowerment Leader

www.ingramcontent.com/pod-product-compliance
Lightning Source LLC
Chambersburg PA
CBHW072213070526
44585CB00015B/1314